A HUMAN BEING
DIED THAT NIGHT

A HUMAN BEING
DIED THAT NIGHT

A South African
Story of Forgiveness

Pumla Gobodo-Madikizela

HOUGHTON MIFFLIN COMPANY
BOSTON • NEW YORK   2003

For information about permission to reproduce selections from
this book, write to Permissions, Houghton Mifflin Company,
215 Park Avenue South, New York, New York 10003.

Visit our Web site: www.houghtonmifflinbooks.com.

Library of Congress Cataloging-in-Publication Data
Gobodo-Madikizela, Pumla, date.
A human being died that night : a South African story
of forgiveness / Pumla Gobodo-Madikizela.
p.   cm.
Includes index.
ISBN 0-618-21189-6
1. De Kock, Eugene. 2. Police—South Africa—Biography.
3. Reconciliation—Political aspects—South Africa. 4. Death
squads—South Africa. 5. Political violence—South Africa.
6. Political persecution—South Africa. 7. Torture—
South Africa. 8. Human rights—South Africa. I. Title.
HV7911.D439 G63 2003
363.2'092—dc21 [B]   2002027564

Printed in the United States of America

Book design by Robert Overholtzer

QUM 10 9 8 7 6 5 4 3 2 1

The epigraph is drawn from the Penguin Classic
edition of *Crime and Punishment,* translated
by David McDuff (1996), p. 595.

For you, Sesi,
in loving memory

Contents

"Brother, brother, what are you saying? I mean, you have blood on your hands!" Dunya cried in despair.

"The blood that's on everyone's hands . . . that flows and has always flowed through the world like a waterfall, that is poured like champagne and for the sake of which men are crowned in the Capitol and then called the benefactors of mankind. Well, just take a closer look and see what's really what!"

— Fyodor Dostoyevsky,
Crime and Punishment

A HUMAN BEING
DIED THAT NIGHT

1 ⩔

Scenes from Apartheid

As I DROVE the last half-mile of the road that leads to South Africa's notorious Pretoria Central Prison, I felt a dread unlike any I had felt in my earlier visits. Before I could make myself ready, a huge sign high above me at the entrance announced the noble agenda: "Correctional Services: Pretoria." The reassuringly professional sign was one of many changes, I half noted, that must have been introduced by the new black director of prisons. I slowed down my car, drove up to within a few yards of the prison entrance, and turned the engine off. I sat there, seeing but not seeing the people milling around gloomily after a visit with loved ones, waiting for the taxi vans that would drive them back to the impoverished townships on the outskirts of Pretoria. My anxiety built until I felt as if it could have exploded through the windows of my car.

The white guard stationed by the prison entrance was by now looking at me suspiciously. I impulsively turned on the ignition, not sure whether to move the car or, as I then decided, to get out, approach the security checkpoint, and announce myself to the guard. Anticipating that he would ask me to spell my name, I handed him my business card. He went to the telephone in his small observation room and returned to tell me that Doreen Krause, the head of the maximum security section of the prison, was expecting me. This hardly came as a relief; by now I needed something — any obstacle — that would give me an excuse to abandon my mission. Farther down the road I could see the massive gray concrete walls of the medium and maximum security sections of the prison.

The last time I'd come here was in 1989 to interview a man on death row for killing a white farmer in the Eastern Cape. There was to be a retrial, and the prisoner's lawyers had asked me to prepare a psychological report on him. That time I had driven straight to the prison without going through Pretoria. Pretoria was a city filled with too many of apartheid's symbols — the Union building, the seat of apartheid's parliament, the statues of Afrikaner heroes, prison cells, and buildings of torture where many opponents of apartheid, black and white, had died or disappeared or mysteriously committed suicide. Pretoria was the heart and soul of apartheid, and I had no desire to set foot there. But now, as I returned to the prison eight years later, Pretoria symbolized something new. It was the city where Nelson Mandela had been inaugurated as the first president of a democratic South Africa. A workforce that reflected this new South Africa had replaced many of the white men and women who had been the civil servants of one of the most brutally repressive systems in modern history. This day, on my way to the Central Prison, I'd driven into Pretoria to experience the atmosphere that came along with this new phase in my country's existence.

I had intended to stop only long enough to pick up some extra batteries for my small tape recorder and to buy coffee before heading for the prison in time for my appointment at noon. Instead, within a few minutes of entering the city, I lost my sense of direction and was driving around in circles through Pretoria's busy streets. It was a surreal scene in which the forbidding architecture of the apartheid era assumed a menacing air and the one-way streets seemed to entangle me in a maze from which I couldn't free myself. Even the jacaranda blooms — trademark of Pretoria's beauty — lining some of the streets into which I strayed couldn't calm me. I stopped three times in the sweltering heat to ask for directions to the prison, on each occasion getting either inadequate or misleading directions. At last help came. At a set of traffic lights on Schubert Street I rolled down my window to take a chance on a middle-aged white Afrikaner motorist in a van. He offered to lead me to the road that would take me to the prison, and I followed him and his ordinary human goodness on my way.

Did I have any weapons in the car? the guard asked. I opened the glove compartment and then the trunk of my car for the security check. Within a few minutes I was driving down the road that led to the maximum security section of the prison, where some of South Africa's most hardened murderers were warehoused. I parked my car and walked toward the massive black metal gates. Inside stood a uniformed black guard who spoke to me through a square opening screened by iron bars. He opened this gate, and as it swung out I took a few steps back. Within seconds I had been escorted inside, and I found myself standing in the middle of a small, dark, stuffy passage with no windows — a checkpoint before visitors were allowed into the main building of the section. Awed, my heart beating hard, I stared at the blank concrete walls and wondered, as I had during my visit eight years before, where the prison's execution chamber was. South Africa had by now scrapped the death penalty. But I couldn't help wondering which corner of the prison apartheid's hangman had presided over. I could see in an adjacent room a guard in uniform, a semiautomatic assault rifle braced smartly against his hefty shoulder. He stepped out and asked me pleasantly what the purpose of my visit was. "Oh, you are the one to see Dikoko."

I was indeed very close to seeing "Dikoko," Eugene de Kock, the man whom many in the country considered the most brutal of apartheid's covert police operatives. "Prime Evil" — his far less familial-sounding nickname — would be more than an abstraction to me within minutes. I was thankful for the presence of the black guard, and amused by his and all the other black guards' mispronunciation of "de Kock" as "Dikoko." As behind-the-scenes engineer of apartheid's murderous operations, he had been faceless and nameless. Now that he was exposed, his name was as unpronounceable — as unspeakable — as his deeds.

Another guard was called, and I was escorted out of the reception room and into a paved area with a small patch of green grass — a rich green that seemed to have been thrown into the midst of the prison gray to shock. My escort and I approached the main maximum security building, the immaculately polished brass trim of its entrance sparkling in the sun. The journey through the prison gates, a total of nine, was not undramatic. Walking through the maze of passages with brightly polished floors — thanks to cheap prison labor — I heard excited shouts and whistling from some black prisoners on a balcony above. They seemed to be enjoying the sight of a female visitor navigating the prison's corridors. Trying not to spoil their fun, I looked up and acknowledged their cheers with a smile. At that moment I felt as if I needed to be cheered more than they did. Finally, leaving behind me the shouting prisoners and noisy keys, each sounding its own note of power at each prison gate, I passed through a metal detector and the last entrance to "C-Max," the section where de Kock was imprisoned. My jitteriness caused me to seize on a second irony. The covert operations unit from which de Kock had commanded fear and power and crafted apartheid's most brutal schemes was the "C" section of the security department. Now he had come to lose that power in the "C" section of the prison, where, as a prisoner categorized as among the most dangerous, he had no privileges, no power.

In C-Max I was walking into a world of even more intense grays — gray walls, gray ceiling, gray floor. In search of some escape from this dull, depressing grayness, my mind wandered to the patch of green I had seen outside. It was an image I would return to many times in my subsequent trips to the prison; the grass stood out in my mind as an invitation to escape from the world of the living dead to that of the living.

The first thing I noticed when I stepped into the room was de Kock's bright orange prison overalls. The color was shocking, so much a part of the scenery I associated with the many prison movies I had seen. *Silence of the Lambs* immediately came to mind, and there was something about that memory that brought a shiver, though its real significance in my meeting with de Kock would emerge two weeks later. As I entered the tiny room, with gray walls and a disproportionately long table and an old leather chair with wheels, de Kock got up, balancing himself against the wall. His feet were chained to a metal stool bolted to the floor. He smiled politely, making eye contact from behind his black-rimmed thick lenses. I could hear the clattering of his leg chains as he awkwardly steadied himself, extending his hand to greet me. He spoke in a heavy Afrikaans accent: "It's a pleasure to meet you." I knew the face; I had seen it in the newspapers, and at public hearings during his first appearance before the Truth and Reconciliation Commission, but this was the closest I had ever been to Eugene de Kock. As he smiled shyly, perhaps politely, rising to greet me, I saw a flicker of boyishness, of uncertainty. At the same time, my mind registered "Prime Evil," the name that marked him as the surest evidence of all that had happened under apartheid. De Kock had not just given apartheid's murderous evil a name. He had *become* that evil. The embodiment of evil stood there politely smiling at me.

I, like every black South African, have lived a life shaped by the violence and the memories of apartheid. I have three linked stories to share.

In 1994 I was completing my doctoral fellowship at Harvard University. On the morning of April 27 I joined the many South Africans assembled at the State House in Boston, where a voting center for South Africans had been created. I was the first person to vote, and my emotions were so intense that I seemed to feel them concretely as something that flooded through me. As I walked to the voting booths, I had an overwhelming sense that I was being transported from one historical moment, where I'd been a second-class citizen in my country of birth — where my parents and their parents had been sent from this place to that, wherever the mass removals and demolitions of black areas destined them to go, finally settling in the nominally independent "homeland" of Transkei — to another historical moment of power, pride, and affirmation. I remember later that day feeling a deep satisfaction, as if I had just completed a difficult race.

When I returned to South Africa in June of that year, on a beautiful clear winter day, I became aware for the fiirst time that in my past travels I could not have described myself as a South African. I could only say that I was *from* South Africa. I remember thinking as my plane landed that day in Cape

Town, This is *my* country, *my* home. Driving from the airport, past Langa Township, where I grew up, with its "informal settlement" sprawl visible from the freeway, I couldn't help recalling that when I was a child living in the township, Cape Town had been out of my reach. As township dwellers, we were Cape Towners in name only. I never truly saw Table Mountain, the epitome of the beauty of this magnificent city, although it is within visual reach of the township; it was part of the world that had tried to strip my people of their dignity and respect, part of the world that had reduced them to second-class citizens in their own country. Langa, like all other South African townships, which were established by the apartheid government as a labor pool for white business, was a world of poverty, where all houses looked alike, each connected to the next like carriages in a long, endless train; where people left their homes to catch early morning trains that took them to the city at dawn; where a history of discrimination, repression, and exclusion from the privileges that citizenship and wealth confer had left its debilitating mark of poverty.

The first time I witnessed a scene of violence, I was five.

On March 21, 1960, a remarkable event occurred that transformed the nature of the anti-apartheid struggle in South Africa. That day several thousand black people gathered in the township of Sharpeville to protest the notorious pass laws requiring blacks to carry internal passports, thus totally regulating their lives. The police opened fire on the crowd, killing 69 and wounding 186, including women and children. Most of the victims were shot in the back while fleeing. The Sharpeville incident was followed by countrywide demonstrations in black townships, leading to more bloodshed. In the township of Langa, the carnage was worse than in Sharpeville.

At least this is how I would remember the events that I witnessed as a little girl of five from behind the hedge of my mother's small garden of our tiny house at 69 Brinton Street.

My memory of the 1960 Langa violence is something I still find difficult to shake out of my mind. Yet its accuracy was tested in 1996 when, as a committee member on South Africa's Truth and Reconciliation Commission, I was forced to revisit the events in Langa Township. What I remembered was the commotion in the row of houses on my street — all replicas of the matchbox structure that was my home. Men I knew as fathers of the girls and boys I played with were running past looking frightened, jumping fences to be anywhere but in their own homes. These were men I referred to as "father," or "so-and-so's father." We never called them by their first names. These were the same fathers you would not want to catch you doing anything wrong in the streets, like playing outside in the dark. Countless times I had shared candy with their children, candy already in my mouth, or in theirs, split and broken into bits inside the mouth so that one, two, or three others could have whatever tiny piece could be shared. These were the men who brought us the candy, but now they were scared and running.

Men I had never seen in my home came out of the coal shed at the back of our house with blackened faces. Some came into the house, moving beds to hide under them, or in closets. Others wore what I later remembered as a look of defiance or impotent rage. My own father was nowhere in sight, and my mother, heavily pregnant with my youngest sister, Sesi, was frantically calling out to the neighbors to try to establish his whereabouts. To escape this chaos of men — scared and defiant men — running in and out of my home, I went outside. There I saw what they were all running away from. Army trucks that looked like huge monsters roamed the streets menacingly, some charging furiously over walkways and into the large field in front of our house to fire into scattered groups of people. Vaguely aware of my elder brother standing behind me, I was witnessing something I had until then never seen before: live shooting, blood, and human death. The image that I was to recall many years later was that of a street covered in blood and bodies lined up like cattle in a slaughterhouse.

The indelible mark left by this incident returned in a flash on June 16, 1976, when I learned that police had on that day massacred over five hundred black students involved in a peaceful march against the imposition of Afrikaans as a language of instruction. When the youthful uprising broke out into violent protest in the Cape Town townships in August of that year, the memory of those bodies, bloodied and dismembered, on Brinton Street sixteen years earlier cried out inside me. At Fort Hare University (which was later closed for the rest of the year), I packed my bags and with other students abandoned my studies to be part of the protests.

Twenty years later, when I was invited to join the Truth and Reconciliation Commission (TRC), I was shocked to learn that what in my memory was a "massacre" had been otherwise. According to archival records, one death had resulted from the police shootings in Langa.

What conclusions can be drawn from what is to me a still haunting discrepancy? How can what I remember so vividly turn out to be unconfirmed by reports of what happened on that day? Since the countrywide protest in 1960 had been organized by the Pan-African Congress (PAC), when the TRC was preparing for its first public hearing in April 1996, I interviewed leaders of the PAC, including its president, Clarence Makwethu, more to straighten out what was irresolvable in my mind than to establish the truth for the records of the

TRC. None of them could confirm what was so very clear in my memory, suggesting that my memory was wrong. Or *was* it? Can what was still so vividly alive in my memory be described simply as a misrepresentation of the facts, a reconstruction and exaggeration of events as they had happened? I asked myself, What does this tell us about remembering traumatic events?

I can only suggest that when the safe world of a child is shattered by the violent invasion of police, the intensity of the moment is something that the experience of a five-year-old cannot absorb. She lacks the psychological capacity to contain the brutality before her eyes, and certainly has no language with which to re-present the traumatic events. *Blood, bodies,* and *death* are the only meaningful words that capture the image of what she cannot truly articulate through language.

Here is my third story.

In 1990 I was lecturing in psychology at the University of Transkei. This was an interesting time in the nominally independent homeland of Transkei. Bantu Holomisa, fondly known as "The General," had recently become leader of Transkei after a bloodless coup. Following the release of Nelson Mandela from prison, Holomisa announced that he was lifting the ban on all political organizations in Transkei. This edict, along with other events in Transkei, angered the South African government, and there was an attempted coup to remove Holomisa from office. Most people at the time, myself included, had no doubt that the apartheid South African government was implicated in the coup attempt. On the day of the incident, all businesses, schools, and other institutions were officially closed. You could see groups of people throughout the city of Umtata, capital of Transkei, their eyes cast upward toward Holomisa's office on the eleventh floor of Botha Sigcau, the tallest building in that small city.

I joined one of the groups that had converged in the streets, watching as the violent drama was unfolding, hoping that whoever was South Africa's agent would not succeed in what he was trying to do. Gunfire echoed in the streets and over our heads, and the smoke and dust pouring from the windows of Botha Sigcau were visible signs of the battle being fought inside. Despite the fact that the action on the eleventh floor was intensifying, despite the fact that it was clear that people could be seriously injured, despite all of that, I was waiting for the moment when I would celebrate victory with those multitudes watching in the streets. The moment of victory did arrive. The officer who was leading the coup attempt, Captain Craig Duli, was "captured." There was jubilation throughout the streets of Umtata. My car was filled to the brim; soldiers perched wherever there was space, hoisting their R1 rifles in the air through the windows as I honked and drove in circles in a spirit of celebration. The soldiers in my car immediately composed a song about how Captain Duli, "puppet of the Boers," couldn't stop Holomisa.

As the true nature of the events emerged, and we heard how the mutilated body of Captain Duli had been thrown into the trunk of an army vehicle, and how he later either died of his wounds or was shot along with others who had sided with him, I realized that I had been party to the killing of another human being. I had knowingly participated in an incident that would certainly result in the taking of a life. In my mind the point was not whether I could have done anything to stop it or not, but simply that I had been there, celebrating.

This was not the end of my shame. In 1996, while serving on the TRC, I was asked by the head of the Eastern Cape branch of the commission, the Reverend Bongani Finca, to be part of the panel that was going to hold a public hearing in Umtata. Before the hearing, each person on the panel was assigned to "facilitate" the testimony of two or more witnesses who would be appearing before the TRC. On similar occasions in the past, when I was not involved in organizing a public hearing, I usually made a point of reading the summaries of the stories of witnesses, and tried whenever possible to meet before the hearing started with those whose testimonies I was assigned to lead. Now I was shocked to see the name of Mrs. Nontobeko Duli, widow of Captain Duli, on the list of people scheduled to testify in Umtata. I did not know how I could sit on a panel and hear her story when only a few years earlier I had celebrated the death of her husband. Here she was, a victim like many others whose stories of trauma I had listened to. How could I with honesty convey words of comfort without first addressing my shame and guilt for having celebrated her husband's death? At the hearing in Umtata, Mrs. Duli was called to the witness stand, and she spoke about her loss, her children, and how she was struggling without the support of her husband. Her pain was as real to me as the rapid beating of my heart.

2 ⟱

An Encounter with "Prime Evil"

MY INTERVIEWS WITH Eugene de Kock began after
his first appearance before the TRC in September 1997, where
he testified about his role in the killing of three black policemen who had died when a bomb exploded in the car they
were driving. De Kock had been an "implicated witness" in
the TRC hearing of five white former security police in Port
Elizabeth who were applying for amnesty for the bombing.
The black policemen, who had been attached to the Motherwell police station in Port Elizabeth, had threatened to expose their white colleagues' involvement in the mysterious
death of four black activists, among whom were the well-
known young anti-apartheid leaders Matthew Goniwe and
Fort Calata. The "Motherwell Bombing," as the incident
came to be known, was ordered by the commander of the police, General Nic van Rensberg, who had approached de Kock
and asked him to "make a plan" for silencing the Motherwell
policemen.

De Kock set out first to design the plan and then to execute it. He approached the technical division of the Pretoria police and instructed them to build a bomb that could be exploded by remote control. De Kock sent some of his men from the apartheid government's death farm, Vlakplaas,[1] to Port Elizabeth "as part of a contingency plan," appointing Riaan Bellingham,[2] he said, to take charge in case something went wrong with the bombing operation.

De Kock testified that the three black policemen were sent on a false mission in a car on which the explosives had secretly been planted. The bomb was set off as planned by remote control, killing the Motherwell policemen, as well as a fourth man, a friend who was in the car with them.

This was de Kock's first appearance before the TRC. As he concluded his testimony, he made an appeal to meet with the widows of the victims of the Motherwell bombing. He wanted to apologize to them but wished to do so privately, he said. I was intrigued by de Kock's request. The boldness of the idea both amazed me and made me curious. Would the widows be willing to see de Kock? What would he say? "I'm sorry I killed your husbands"?

The widows' lawyer agreed to the meeting. Present were two of the widows, Pearl Faku and Doreen Mgoduka, their lawyer, de Kock, and his lawyer, Schalk Hugo.

A few days later I met with Mrs. Mgoduka and Mrs. Faku during a weekend of debriefing. "I was profoundly touched by him," Mrs. Faku said of her encounter with de Kock. Both women felt that de Kock had communicated to them something he felt deeply and had acknowledged their pain. "I couldn't control my tears. I could hear him, but I was overwhelmed by emotion, and I was just nodding, as a way of saying yes, I forgive you. I hope that when he sees our tears, he knows that they are not only tears for our husbands, but tears for him as well. . . . I would like to hold him by the hand, and show him that there is a future, and that he can still change."[3]

The image of the widow reaching out to her husband's murderer struck me as an extraordinary expression — and *act* — of empathy, to shed tears not only for her loss but also, it seemed, for the loss of de Kock's moral humanity. Was de Kock deserving of the forgiveness shown him? Was he too evil — "*Prime* Evil" — to be worthy of the forgiveness Mrs. Faku and Mrs. Mgoduka had offered him? Was evil intrinsic to de Kock, and forgiveness therefore wasted on him?

Faku and Mgoduka's response to the mastermind of their husbands' deaths was what led me to my meeting with de Kock, and to the fundamental questions surrounding remorse and forgiveness after mass atrocity which are raised in this book. If showing compassion to our enemies is something that our bodies recoil from, what should our attitude be to their cries for mercy, the cries that tell us their hearts are breaking, and that they are willing to renounce the past and their role in it? How can we transcend hate if the goal is to transform human relationships in a society with a past marked by violent conflict between groups?

This question may be irrelevant for people who do not have to live as a society with their former enemies. But for those whose lives are intertwined with those who have grossly violated human rights, who sometimes even have to live as neighbors with them, ignoring the question is not an option. Not closing the door to understanding may be one of the ways in which people can redefine their understanding of atrocities and see them as something that is, like evil in the self, always a possibility in any political system that has emerged from a violent past. There are countless examples in history of government by people who have risen out of oppressive rule to become oppressors themselves.

When violators of human rights allow themselves to be emotionally vulnerable, they are giving others a chance to encounter them as human beings. When this happens, it is inevitable for one to wonder: If they can *feel* like human beings, if they can share a human moment with those on whom they inflicted trauma, pain, and misery, why did the good side of humanity fail when it was needed most? Hannah Arendt's much-used phrase "the banality of evil" has frequently been offered as explanation, as if it revealed all the complexities of what constitutes evil. Encountering those who were once engineers of evil in state-sponsored atrocities may provide important lessons on how "monsters" are produced in a political system that uses repressive violence to achieve its ends.

Attempting to understand the perpetrators of evil has deeply disturbing implications. Christopher Browning, who studied men who had been part of a battalion sent to Poland to carry out the massacre of Jews, suggests that understanding implies an attempt to empathize. But, he says, "what I do not accept, however, are the old clichés that to explain is to excuse, to understand is to forgive."[4] To what extent does the attempt to understand "explain away" the behavior of murderers? When we locate causes "out there" — in society and in structures of authority — does this not implicitly make violent acts more acceptable to the mind? Does understanding not send an implicit message of mercy born out of compassion for the murderer in view of the circumstances found to have influenced his behavior?

The issue of "understanding" perpetrators has often been a contentious one, and the question "to understand or not to understand" has led some to conclude that people who are responsible for unspeakable tragedy are not worthy of any kind of examination by scholars. Emile Fackenheim has devised the concept of a "double move," which is to "seek an explanation but also to resist explanation."[5] This is probably the metaphor that best captures the tension, contradiction, and complexity that are forever present when one comes face-to-face with the coexistence of good and evil in human beings. Ron Rosenbaum elaborates on the significance of Fackenheim's paradox and explains that it means "not to resist all or any inquiry . . . but to resist the misleading exculpatory corollaries of explanation. To resist the way explanation can become an evasion or consolation."[6] Some take the extreme view and suggest that no language should be created to understand evil, that to do so would be committing an "obscenity."[7]

And so it was finally that single encounter, one that raised burning questions for me, which led to my interviews with de Kock, a series of meetings that amounted to forty-six hours over a period of six months.

Both of us seated, I asked de Kock to tell me about his first appearance before the TRC. "Well, I sat through the first two days of the hearing," he said. "I didn't know what to expect, and I wasn't sure how it would be when I stepped on stage. At first I was, how can I put it? A little — " he paused, searching for an appropriate word — "nervous. But once I started talking, it was like shedding a cloak." And as he said this, he moved his shoulders up, then down, gesturing with his hands as if enacting the removal of something from his shoulders. "It brought a lot of relief," he said.

As de Kock described his first appearance before the commission's public hearing, I thought about how close I had come to abandoning the idea of interviewing him, and how all of my doubts were beginning to be irrelevant. I thought about what it should mean to be sitting in a small, enclosed space with the most notorious executor of apartheid's most brutal methods of repression, the commander of the headquarters for the "dirty war" waged by the apartheid government against its enemies in the African National Congress (ANC), the Pan-African Congress (PAC), and their allies. De Kock, I knew, was the kind of commander who did not issue orders from behind an office desk. He went out with his men on many murderous operations. He had been at the center of the chaos, the blood, the bodies, and the killing, directing it. But here I was, feeling little of what I thought I was supposed to feel, and listening to de Kock as he tried to articulate his own feelings about an event that promised him freedom, if not actual, at least of the emotional kind.

Earlier in the day the head of C-Max, Doreen Krause, had confirmed the image of evil and danger attached to de Kock. She had briefed me before my meeting with him, "to prepare you and make sure you understand the safety precautions." De Kock, Krause told me, was already in the room, in chains. This precaution reflected his jailers' opinion of him, clearly articulated in a public statement issued on South African national television by the commissioner of correctional services, Khulekani Sithole, that de Kock had "an evil profile."[8] Krause continued to explain that I was expected to exercise caution. I should keep sharp objects away from de Kock to make sure he couldn't reach out and grab them to use as weapons. The prison had provided me with a chair on wheels, which I could scoot back with ease in the event of an attack by de Kock. Krause had been standing throughout the briefing, but when she came to the detail about the chair as a vehicle of escape, she sat down in her own office chair and demonstrated the escape with a swift backward push. I was struck by her physical appearance. She seemed an incongruous person to be heading a prison wing where the most dangerous of South Africa's criminals were serving their sentences. She was a small blond woman with a pleasant disposition. She wore the standard-issue brown warder's uniform, with a belt that emphasized her trim waistline, and calf-high boots that made her look more like a trendy mountain climber than the head of C-Max. She stood out among her junior colleagues, black and white, whose shapes and sizes were unremarkable. Then, too, she spoke with a heavy Afrikaans accent, which never fails to trigger a memory in me of the bad old days of apartheid. I listened to her describe the restrictions on her former government's most valued secret operative and thought how she and de Kock had once been working for the same side.

As my first conversation with de Kock progressed, I noticed no signs of the overt dangerousness I had been warned about during the briefing (not that dangerousness is a clearly understood concept, even with psychological measurement).⁰ There was another reality that was about to be unveiled about de Kock, one that reflected a struggle of a deeply personal nature and that showed just how complex his life of violence had been, and how unsatisfactory reducing it to a single label was. When de Kock spoke about his past, his recollections seemed to reflect some of the same factors that led others to reduce him to a label. There were times when he described details of his violent past with a vividness that was frightening. He had belonged to a world that created violence, I to a world that was the object of this violence; he belonged to a world where morality meant the same thing as hate, and I to a world that knew the difference. Our worlds were the black and white of lies and truth, and yet as de Kock spoke, the boundaries of our worlds did not always seem so clear.

"Essentially you had 4 million people [whites] trying to keep 40 million people [blacks] in line through wars fought inside and outside the country — of course, not the conventional kind of war," de Kock said when I asked him to explain the extent of the violence and covert operations used by the government during the apartheid era.

"But you know how they do it — I mean, you don't do it by always smiling and being a nice guy, you have to be honest about that. And I was right in the middle of it. I've been in all of these wars. The only thing I haven't been involved in is conventional warfare. I mean, I was as close to it as you can get, but I can tell you that the dirtiest war you can ever get is the one fought in the shadows. And I was there in the middle of it. There are no rules except to win. There are no lines drawn to mark where you cannot cross. So you can go very low — I mean very low — and it still doesn't hit you. It's not like you stop and think. No. Your goal is to get it done. The codes that those people fighting in the shadows will have will be the codes that are inherently — that they came out of their homes with, they grew up with."

De Kock often spoke in general terms when he was relating a personal experience. I understood his reference to codes of behavior being inherent as a reference to his home environment. De Kock's father, a magistrate, seems to have had a far greater influence on de Kock than he was willing to acknowledge. De Kock described his father as a staunch Afrikaner nationalist who was "strongly anticommunist." He was a member of the Broederbond (the Solidarity of Brotherhood), a secret Afrikaner society composed of politicians, high-ranking government officials, religious leaders, judges, bankers, businesspeople, and academics. The Broederbond may very well have no equivalent in the twentieth-century history of political organizations. Both the Soviet Communist Party and the German Nazi Party bear some similarity to it, since both parties dominated the political, economic, social, and cultural lives of the Soviet Union and Germany, respectively. But unlike in the Broederbond, membership in these two parties was not reserved exclusively for people in high-level leadership positions in all sectors of civil society. The Communist Party and the Nazi Party were also not secret societies; membership was proudly and publicly declared. There are some parallels between the Broederbond and the Ku Klux Klan, including the goals of white Afrikaner supremacy, the use of propaganda intrinsic to the goals of nationalism, and the ritually enforced secrecy.[10]

The secrecy of the Broederbond makes it one of the most sinister organizations that operated during the period of apartheid rule because it is difficult to know to what extent its functioning affected people's lives. In his youth in the 1960s, de Kock and his brother, his only sibling, were fed a rich diet of Afrikaner nationalism. In 1960, when the ANC declared an armed struggle after five decades of peaceful protest against apartheid, the government denounced it as a communist threat.[11] To the theme of Afrikaner nationalism was added that of anticommunism. De Kock recounted how these refrains dominated dinner conversations among the adults who came to his home and were constant themes within the families he was acquainted with. These were probably the early influences that led de Kock to believe that he had the duty to engage in activities that enforced apartheid policy and protected the supremacy of the Afrikaner nation. Interestingly, de Kock's father equated Afrikaner nationalism with the ANC's struggle for liberation. As a nationalist, his father had said to him, had he been black, he would have joined the ANC.

I watched de Kock as he relished this thought of the parallels between apartheid's Afrikaner nationalism and the ANC's struggle, with the only significant difference between the two being racial composition. (What is missing in this analogy, of course, is the ANC's policy of non-racialism.) De Kock explained that, although he was an Afrikaner nationalist and a member of the Broederbond, his father was never a racist, that he spoke more than one African language "fluently" and would sometimes correct a court interpreter if he were given an incorrect translation of testimony in one of the African languages he understood. De Kock's attempt to establish the legitimacy of Afrikaner nationalism by invoking his father's imagining himself as a black member of the ANC seemed quite laughable to me. It reminded me of a frustrating conversation Peter Malkin had with Adolf Eichmann in Argentina before Eichmann was flown to Jerusalem to be tried there. Malkin, the Israeli secret policeman who actually captured Eichmann in 1960, describes the many hours he spent with the former Nazi commander of Auschwitz in his book *Eichmann in My Hands*. In one conversation, Eichmann makes an argument that bears a striking resemblance to what de Kock told me. "You must believe me," Malkin recalls Eichmann's explaining to him, "I was always an idealist. Had I been born Jewish, I'd have been the most fervent Zionist!" He even goes on to tell Malkin that he studied Hebrew "with a Rabbi in Berlin."[12]

This is a trick most perpetrators use, especially those sponsored by a powerful government, to try to make their actions understandable by saying, "What my people have done, yours have done too." What is tragic is that they really do believe that what they have done is no worse than the other group's actions. Typically, the perpetrator starts off with rationalization, to convince himself of the legitimacy of his acts, then he begins to communicate his rationalization to others. At this point it is no longer a rationalization but a "truth" that releases the perpetrator from any sense of guilt he may still feel about his evil deeds. If the enemy is doing the same thing he himself is engaged in, then he can't be that bad.

De Kock knew that what he had done as commander of covert police activity at Vlakplaas was simply beyond what most human beings could understand. When it came down to it, it was beyond what *he* could understand, once he was removed from the day-to-day demands of the destructive life he had led. And this was his burden, his struggle. The cloak had now been removed to reveal what had been hidden before, not only from the public eye but from himself as well. This presence of an inner stirring within de Kock is, as I will show, what marks the fundamental difference between him and his former colleagues who appeared before the TRC, as well as between him and Eichmann. Some people, when faced with their evil deeds, understand the moral implications of their actions, but to maintain some "dignity," to protect their sense of identity as respectable human beings, they cling to the belief that what they did was morally correct. One can get a sense that they are struggling with their denial of the truth. But with Eichmann, the evidence suggests, there was just blankness, a blank, impenetrable wall.

It has been pointed out that some of the most notorious Nazis "liked" children. For example, Robert Lifton, who interviewed Nazi doctors who conducted "medical experiments" in Auschwitz, points out that Josef Mengele, the most notorious of these "experimenters," would walk around with children, play with them, and give them lollipops as he led them to their death. De Kock's conscience regarding children led him to respond differently. He protected them. "I made it very clear verbally," he told me with passion, "and in virtually every operation you don't, you don't harm children." De Kock laid an emphasis on the "don't" and gave a simultaneous shaking of his head for further emphasis to show how strongly he felt about this. If any of his men were to kill a child, he said, he would personally execute them. He continued, "You will find that some people will have no problem killing out the whole household: man, woman, and child. But in my operations I said, 'Leave the women and children.'" He was boastful about this (strikingly incomplete) code of conscience.

There had been so many "cross-border operations"[13] in which both women and children were killed that I found it hard to believe that de Kock had tried to protect children. I asked him if he maintained this standard in all of his operations. "Well, sometimes women were themselves armed, and in such cases the woman was an equal, because she could potentially cause harm. So there was no choice but to treat her like the others. There is one case, which I deeply regret, where two children did get harmed. They got killed, which I still see today as a blot on what I had strived for."

If protecting children in his operations was what de Kock "strived for," I wondered if he went out of his way to determine whether children would be present, or if he simply stumbled upon children and then commanded his men to act accordingly. If the former were the case, it would reflect a deeply held moral principle, in a perverse sort of way. It would also suggest that perhaps he had a conception of his professional role as inconsistent with harming innocent children. Harming helpless and unarmed people, however, was part of the code of "the war in the shadows"; there were no rules, as he had told me. So how, I asked, did this code concerning the protection of children fit in with the idea of a war fought in the shadows? There were limits, he said. And his limits involved not harming children. The incident that he regretted, in which two children were killed, took place in Botswana, where he was sent by the head of the police, General Nic van Rensberg, on a secret mission with other police officers to kill a couple who were working as double agents, helping PAC guerrillas returning to South Africa to conduct bombing operations, and working as spies for the military.[14] "I just did not have information," he explained. "It's not an excuse, but that information just was not there." I asked him if he would have refused to go had he known that children would be in danger. "The operation would have gone ahead, but the children wouldn't have got killed."

I was not convinced that de Kock's policy of protecting children had arisen purely out of moral concerns. But could it be true that de Kock had in fact gone out of his way to save children? I later arranged an interview with Arnold Nofemela, a former member of the death squads that were under de Kock's command at Vlakplaas. One of apartheid's notorious hit squad operatives, Nofemela had come to the public's attention in 1989 when he blew the whistle on the secret activities at Vlakplaas. At the time he was on death row in Pretoria Prison for the murder of a white farmer during a robbery that had nothing to do with his Vlakplaas activities.

Nofemela confirmed that de Kock tried to protect children from harm in his deadly missions. He remembered an inci dent in one cross-border operation in which a child suddenly appeared screaming fearfully and ran up and down the corridor where de Kock and his quarry were exchanging gunfire. The shooting stopped out of concern for the safety of the child. De Kock also related an incident to me in which he had placed a child in a separate room from where he and his men had just killed ANC members and telephoned the police to inform them about the child survivor of the incident. If de Kock was capable of so much evil, as the evidence of his past shows, how could he have found the compassion to save children from the tragic consequences of his actions? Was something more psychologically subtle going on, something that perhaps had to do with his childhood, his helplessness as a child and his own need for protection?

One of the things that struck me during my hours of conversation with de Kock was how well the apartheid government had concealed its work from ordinary citizens. This lends some small degree of credibility to the defense of South Africa's whites who say that they didn't know what was going on, that the government hid much of it from them. The government's security and intelligence systems operated through a secret network of informants, "a totally interwoven shield," de Kock called it, "stretching all the way up into the ANC's high-ranking membership."[15] Many of the black informants were *askaris*, former ANC and PAC members who had fled the country but were then captured while attempting to reenter South Africa to launch bombing operations.

I asked de Kock how he and his team had recruited them. "Blackmail," he said, "especially for whites — if you know of an extramarital affair, prostitutes, or something that will embarrass them."

"Did you use a different set of tactics to get blacks to inform for you?" I asked.

"Well, people are different. You can't threaten a black person with the prospect of exposing an extramarital affair. It doesn't work. Blacks are used to this kind of thing. Same thing with many European countries. They don't care about extramarital affairs. Money — yes. Money is usually the main thing, especially if you want the important people."

"Why is that?" I asked.

"Well, there are two groups. The big guys. You tap the phones of family members, intercept their mail, that sort of thing. And you find out about the situation at home. So you offer money in exchange for information. There was a lot of money to offer these people. Then there are the *askaris*. Those kinds are captured, and then they join our side."

"And, of course, they come to Vlakplaas," he added, with little trace of the horror contained in the statement. "Some of them just came to us; they are maybe tired of the ill-treatment in the ANC camps. They were severely tortured by the ANC in the camps. That came out at the [TRC] hearings, but we knew this all along. So as I said, some of them came to Vlakplaas of their own free will."

"What about those who were captured? How did you change their will? How did you convert them?"

"Well, you usually asked some questions —"

I waited for some elucidation of what this meant, knowing his penchant for understatement whenever he became uncomfortable discussing the most sinister layers of the government's strategy against anti-apartheid activists and his role in it. None was forthcoming.

I tried to prod him. "You mean *interrogated*?"

De Kock turned his eyes away and shifted in his seat, a response I observed over and over, especially when he wanted to avoid a particular line of questioning or was being less than truthful. It was not as if de Kock thought he could hide information about his past. Most of it was already available through the records of his trial, and he had revealed even the most gruesome details of his life story in a book written by

Jeremy Gordin.[16] I think de Kock's discomfort concerning the details had something to do with my being a woman; or perhaps he perceived my sympathy for him and was afraid that if we focused on the gory particulars of his past, he would lose it. Clearly he didn't want to admit that he and his men had used torture methods to "bring around" captured *askaris* and force them into the dirty operations of the security police.

"The real question was: now were they better off at Vlakplaas than where they were? I don't know. But when they came to us they were broken, if not spiritually, physically," he said contemptuously.[17]

"What were the rules? Were *askaris* allowed to return to their original organizations? Were they expected to spy on one another as they moved in and out of Vlakplaas?"

"*Askaris* were free to move as they pleased. But they had to be careful not to be found out. They came back when they had to."

"What if they didn't return?" I asked.

"Well, they were free to move about," he replied, sounding agitated. "They could go back to the ANC if they wanted to. We never stopped them. *I* didn't stop them. It was their choice to stay. And maybe that's what they preferred, I don't know."

This was obviously not true. Johannes Mabotha, a member of the ANC's armed wing, became an *askari* after he tried to return to South Africa on a secret anti-apartheid mission. After Mabotha had been arrested, tortured, and forced to become a government agent, he managed to escape from Vlakplaas and joined a group aligned with the ANC. Mabotha was hunted down and arrested again. He was interrogated and tortured by the Soweto Security Branch and by de Kock and his men. Then they took him to an unused asbestos mine northeast of Johannesburg, where de Kock shot him. They tied explosives to his body and blew him up. There were others who were killed, apparently for trying to desert Vlakplaas, such as Moses Nthehelang and Brian Ngqulunga.[18]

Once captured and "converted," *askaris* were pressed into service on covert missions ranging from spying on their own comrades to abduction and murder. So effective was the Vlakplaas spy network that security departments throughout South Africa used it, often with the tacit support or outright connivance of cabinet-level politicians. In 1985, for example, Johannes Velde van der Merwe, second in command of the Security Branch of the East Rand Police, formulated a plan to "eliminate" members of the Congress of South African Students (COSAS). With the full support of General Johannes Coetzee, the commissioner of police, and the approval of Louis Le Grange, the minister of police, van der Merwe assembled a contingent of police, technical staff, and *askaris* from Vlakplaas. The rest of the team consisted of Paul Jacobus Hattingh, commander of the Explosives and Demolition Division of the East Rand Security Branch, Wybrand Lodewicus du Toit of the Technical Division of the Security Branch, and Eugene de Kock.[19]

The team devised its plan. Two *askaris*, Joe Mamasela and Daniel Nkalato, posing as members of the ANC's military wing who had returned to South Africa to rejoin the struggle, were to infiltrate a targeted group of twenty student activists and train them in the use of explosives. On June 25, 1985, the anniversary of the adoption of the ANC's Freedom Charter, the *askaris* supplied the students with hand grenades and sent them out to bomb a predetermined target. Unbeknownst to the trainees, the timing devices in the grenades had been set to zero seconds. They would go off in their hands the moment the pins were pulled.

In the explosions that followed, thirteen were killed instantly. Seven survived but were severely injured and, on top of that, were arrested on charges of terrorism and the unlawful possession of hand grenades. François Steenkamp, an explosives expert attached to the East Rand Security Branch, conducted the police investigation of the incident. As the state investigator, Steenkamp of course knew exactly what had happened and why the grenades had gone off but for twelve years kept this covert information confidential until he was summoned before the Truth Commission in 1997 to testify under protection of the amnesty law.[20] In the language of apartheid, de Kock explained to me, this kind of operation was referred to as "preemptive killing." You move in to kill rather than arrest your victims before they can cause any destruction.[21] This, however, is not what whites were told about this incident through the national newspapers and television. They were told that "communists" had been killed by their own bombs, that the government was succeeding in rooting them out and stopping them in their tracks. "Preemptive killing" at the time was designed to build trust among white voters and to show apartheid politicians that the country's security police were doing their job efficiently.

"We had to be seen to be on top of the ANC threat at all costs," de Kock explained. "If there was a lot of trouble in an area, I would send my men to contact sources to come over. We would start phoning, say, a chap, a source, back in Botswana. We would cover all bases in order to hit back hard. At the same time — you see, there had to be something happening."

"So there was pressure from your superiors for the security department to show results?" I asked.

"No," he said, though this did not mean that he was disagreeing with me. De Kock sometimes began his responses with "no" even if he meant yes, as if he felt it was a safe policy to start with a denial before proceeding.

"No, it was always, you know, pressure. I can remember Colonel Johan Coetzee, or General Johan Coetzee, and Johan van der Merwe going raving mad one day, shouting: 'We are paying millions and millions every month. Where are the targets? I want a target now. I want a target within the next twenty minutes. The target must be attacked. Don't tell me you don't have targets, you don't have information. Where do all the millions go?' You must remember *they* had the politicians on their backs. They had to show them that their policy of *kragdadigheid* [strong-arm tactics] was working."[22]

Nobody could say what the budget allocated to Vlakplaas was, but it was calculated that the slush fund used to pay off local and international informants and assassins and to pay for weapons, cover-up operations, and overseas and cross-border trips ran into the millions of rand.

"So you had to *organize* targets?" I asked.

"No, basically, they wanted results. We had to keep those operations going, inside and outside the country, to keep voters happy, to show them that the government can protect them from the onslaught of the liberation forces. I had no problem with this. If there was an explosion at the Wimpy Bar that killed women and children, we had to hit back. If these people were setting up bombs to kill innocent civilians, women and children, then I had no problem with the operations," he said defensively.

By killing, de Kock and his colleagues were not just protecting the government — killing for "the state" — but were so deep into these operations that they were now killing to protect themselves. Vlakplaas became de Kock's life. By the time stories about the true nature of his activities at Vlakplaas began to surface, he had become a driven killer with an impressive trail of violent murders behind him. There were others like him, decent men who had been charged with the country's security and the protection of its citizens — which, under the circumstances, inevitably meant its white citizens. Slowly, they became murderers.

I asked de Kock to talk about the meeting with Pearl Faku and Doreen Mgoduka. His face immediately fell, and he became visibly distressed. I could hear the clatter of his leg chains as he shuffled his feet. Sitting directly across from me in the small prison consulting room, his heavy glasses on the table that separated us, he started to speak. There were tears in his eyes. In a breaking voice he said: "I wish I could do much more than [say] I'm sorry. I wish there was a way of bringing their bodies back alive. I wish I could say, 'Here are your husbands,'" he said, stretching out his arms as if bearing an invisible body, his hands trembling, his mouth quivering, "but unfortunately . . . I have to live with it."

Relating to him in the only way one does in such human circumstances, I touched his shaking hand, surprising myself. But it was clenched, cold, and rigid, as if he were holding back, as if he were holding on to some withering but still vital form of his old self. This made me recoil for a moment and to recast my spontaneous act of reaching out as something incompatible with the circumstances of an encounter with a person who not too long ago had used these same hands, this same voice, to authorize and initiate unspeakable acts of malice against people very much like myself.

And yet, immersed as I was in the concrete circumstances of a prison interview room, sitting across from a trembling man in chains, something else seemed to assure me that there was nothing especially incongruous in his display of emotional vulnerability and my response. I tried as best I could to carry on normally, to maintain my professional composure. And yet I felt guilty for having expressed even momentary sympathy and wondered if my heart had actually crossed the moral line from compassion, which allows one to maintain a measure of distance, to actually identifying with de Kock.

In my confusion about what had just happened I was startled to hear the guard: "You are way over the time limit, *suster,*" he said from behind me. He used the familiar but respectful *suster* (sister) that most young black men in the townships use to address women in an older but comparatively close age group. His words increased the conflict but also came as a relief. The professional side of me felt that there was something thoughtless and uncaring about leaving de Kock at the point where the conversation had taken him. But the confusion unleashed by my touching de Kock was becoming too much to bear, and I was relieved that I didn't have to stay.

It was 3.25 P.M. When Doreen Krause had given me my briefing almost four hours earlier, she had said that I had to be out by 3:00. At the time I was secretly amused that she had thought to mention time restrictions. It was unthinkable that I could spend more than two hours with de Kock, let alone three and a half. The walk back to my car through the prison gates and long passages, which were by now quiet, seemed longer than when I'd come that morning. Walking into the sunshine, I felt free. The small patch of green grass — what a relief it was to be touched by that tiny patch of bright color in the sun! It was as if I were breathing for the first time. But as I drove out of the prison toward Johannesburg, I started to feel a great sense of anxiety and despair. During my drive, I suddenly broke down in sobs. Here I was, a woman sobbing alone in a car on the N1 freeway. My emotions were becoming increasingly confused, but only in the sense that they represented my multiple identities, the past, and the present: as a child, student, and adult growing up under the apartheid regime; as a human being able to feel compassion for the suffering of others; as a member of the Truth and Reconciliation Commission expected to remain levelheaded in my thinking about the past.

My tears were for all those years of being denied the right to share a sense of pride about being South African, and being relegated to a second-class citizen, even a foreigner, in the country of my birth, and my parents' and their parents' birth. I felt a deep sense of loss about this. But at the same time, I felt a sense of loss about de Kock, that the side of him I had touched had not been allowed to triumph over the side that made him apartheid's killing machine. That moment back in the interview room gave me a glimpse of what he could have been. Hard as the memory of having touched him was, the experience made me realize something I was probably not prepared for — that good and evil exist in our lives, and that evil, like good, is always a possibility. And that was what frightened me.

Alone on the N1 to Johannesburg, I was angry at the blindness that characterized a country in which all black people were forced into the status of second-class citizenship, a blindness that has come to be associated with societies that have suffered mass trauma. I was angry that the same society that had created de Kock, that had accepted his murderous protection of their privilege, had ostracized him and was now standing in judgment of him.

I was aware of an increasing grip of fear both within and without. As I was driving on the freeway I felt an urge to glance in the rear-view mirror every now and again — the rear-view mirror had never seemed more important in my twenty-one years of driving. As I approached the exit for Johannesburg, I was shocked to discover that it had taken me twenty minutes to drive a distance that normally took me thirty-five.

What was I running away from? De Kock? His ghosts? Or mine? As I pondered these questions, I remembered having had similar feelings of flight a few months earlier. I'd been driving out of Westville Prison in Durban after an interview with one of the black hit squad members abandoned by his organization, the Inkatha Freedom Party (IFP), the right-wing group that was known to collaborate with apartheid security forces to destroy the ANC wherever it was active. I usually asked perpetrators their ages but wouldn't concern myself with their birth dates. But I found myself asking Gcina Hlongwane, who had told me he had killed so many ANC members he couldn't tell the exact number, about his birthday. It turned out to be the same as mine. I was dumbfounded. I had to steady myself just to consider what it meant to share something so personal with a man whom many would consider a mass murderer. Normally when one finds out that one shares a birthday with someone, the reaction is, "Oh, really, that's my birthday too!" The response is meant to bond two people who may be strangers. But how could I say this? How could I admit to having something as personal as my birthday in common with him? I remained in this state of confusion until the conversation drifted into substantive matters. It wasn't long before a senior white prison official walked into the room where I was interviewing Hlongwane. Before I could exchange greetings with the man, Hlongwane bent forward and touched my shoe, mumbling something in Zulu. It took me a moment to realize that he was speaking in code, warning me to change the subject in the presence of the white officer because, Hlongwane said, he was a member of the IFP. Once more I froze at the somehow surreal thought that I could be speaking in coded language with this man, that he could take me into his world of secrets and private language, and that I was becoming a part of that world, alone with him, leaving others outside a conversation that only he and I could understand.

The road just out of Westville Prison is not a good road to be on if you are harboring fears. It's not a very long stretch, but it feels desolate, with overgrown grass flanking the roadway. I was reminded of how I had stepped on the accelerator as I drove up the winding road just outside Westville Prison, trying to escape from imaginary men — white men with guns, black men with "cultural weapons" who were lying in hiding in the thick grass by the side of the road. My fears had evoked the racial stereotypes portrayed on television of axe-wielding blacks and whites with "sophisticated" weaponry. But then again this was also the reality in the Durban area at the time of apartheid's collaboration with the IFP.

Approaching Johannesburg, I decided that I wouldn't drive straight to the airport to catch my flight to Cape Town, but would stop to spend the night with my friend Kedi. I felt that I needed to be surrounded by friends. People who were doing regular jobs and had husbands and lovers and children. People who at the end of a day's work went home and were greeted by the usual smell of their homes, and who went to sleep easily at night — people who inhabited the world I was familiar with.

3 ⬇

The Trigger Hand

IN THE WEEKS following my trip to C-Max, details of de Kock's deeds were paraded in the press and on television. Jacques Pauw's documentary *Prime Evil* was screened on national television, allowing the South African public to see just how depraved de Kock and his cronies were. The image I'd been carrying of a chained de Kock sitting in a small prison chair, trembling and breaking down, was replaced by one of him as the evil one, merciless, lashing out violently at his victims, instilling fear and silencing them. I had visions of him building bombs and testing them on pigs' heads before blowing off those of his human victims. He was scrutinizing hit lists, designing murderous plots in dark offices, hiding explosives in letters, pens, and headphones to send to the next victim, and to the next, and the next. He was the death terror, his face full of venom, screaming abuse at victims, assaulting and killing them in a rage. I saw de Kock in my tortured mind's eye in his most vicious state — as *prime evil*. These images were too difficult to take in, too much to comprehend, even if

I could imagine them. I had to remind myself that if it was that difficult for me, how much worse it must have been for the people who had faced the evil directly and been destroyed because of it. Here I was, reaching out with my human hand to touch the physical body that had made evil happen.

I had seen his other side, where I had shared a common idiom of humanity with him, and I needed to find out how and why it had been silenced. By the time I met de Kock again, I was ready to see reality as it had been revealed to me: two sides of de Kock, one evil, and the other — the one I was more afraid of confronting — a human being capable of feeling, crying, and knowing pain.

Whenever a public hearing was to be held on the ninth floor at 106 Adderly, on Cape Town's main street, where the TRC had its offices, it always seemed as if a major human drama were about to be launched. There were gangs of reporters with their TV cameras and sophisticated photographic equipment, high-level security police milling about, bag scanners — and, if someone like de Kock were appearing, body scanners as well — TRC personnel, logistics officers, investigators carrying bulging files, judges walking the corridors, godlike, and spectators. On this particular occasion, de Kock had been "invited" by the TRC to attend the amnesty hearing for an incident in which he had been implicated. He himself was not expected to testify. As I sat in my office on the seventh floor that day, a rather amused TRC staff member came to tell me that de Kock was asking for me. It was during an adjournment in the public hearings. The staff member chuckled as he asked why I would have a rendezvous "with Prime Evil." De Kock's call for me had created quite a stir. As I walked past the reception area, where some TRC members had converged casually, remarks were passed playfully about my being "friends with Evil."

I found de Kock in the room reserved for perpetrators' tea and lunch breaks. He was standing in front of an urn with a cup in his hand, surrounded by prison guards whose watchful eyes were everywhere else but on de Kock. Our eyes met, and he was clearly pleased to see me. Wearing his olive green prison clothes, he looked more like a policeman than a prisoner. I wondered if de Kock had called for me out of a need to escape from the gory confessions he had sat through earlier that morning, which told of a grim world he'd once inhabited. He rushed through the obligatory exchange of greetings like a man with something more important to talk about. With an intent look on his face, he thanked me "for the other day," a reference to our meeting in the prison interview room. Then, with an expression that seemed to reflect genuine amazement, he said, "You know, Pumla, that was my trigger hand you touched."

I have not, up until now, been able to free myself from the grip of that statement nor to soften its visceral impact. It was a remark pregnant with so many confusing and contradictory messages. It seemed to unveil the dark pleasures of a man who, at one point, not only had enjoyed inflicting considerable pain on others but also had perhaps relished imagining and reimagining how they must have felt, and had drawn strength and pride from watching others express revulsion when he regaled them with graphic stories from the field. Standing in the corner of this tearoom, faced with de Kock and surrounded by some of his former comrades in murder and by their lawyers, de Kock had not betrayed any obvious malice in his face or tone of voice; but perhaps he was too professional a killer for that. Did he speak those words in the tones of a self-shaming confessional, the cry of a leper in ancient times shouting, "Unclean! Unclean!"? Or with the depraved relish of a Hannibal Lecter making a voyeuristic foray into the mind of a black woman? I couldn't say.[1]

De Kock certainly had succeeded in making short shrift of any sort of boundary between interviewer and subject. He had penetrated my defenses. I felt invaded, naked, angry. It was hard to believe that in the days following my prison visit, while I had been struggling with emotions of sympathy and empathy, *he* had been thinking about — no, plotting — ways to spook me, to gain the upper hand by stemming the momentum of my moral crusade. Yet my act had been unpremeditated; my intentions had been sincere. The unfairness, the sheer asymmetry of it, left me feeling as if the rug had been pulled out from under me.

In touching de Kock's hand I had touched his leprosy, and he seemed to be telling me that, even though I did not realize it at the time, I was from now on infected with the memory of having embraced into my heart the hand that had killed, maimed, and blown up lives. It was as if he wanted to make sure, to insist, that if I intended to visit his cell and talk with him, then I should have the courage to do it not by retreating behind the professional facade of the Truth Commission's ritualized, courtlike proceedings but with the full knowledge that in engaging him, I was engaging a man who still carried evil with him. He wanted his evil to be real to me because it was still real to him.

I had not immediately felt a chill when I touched de Kock. But something odd did happen the morning after the interview. I was awake and lying in bed. Then it dawned on me that I couldn't lift my right forearm. I immediately "knew" why. It was the same hand with which I had reached out to offer consolation to de Kock, and now it had gone completely numb. I couldn't feel with it, as if my body were rejecting a foreign organ illegitimately planted. I tried again. For a long, anxious moment it felt disabled, grounded, as if placed on probation for engaging in a prohibited act.

De Kock, I came to see, seemed also to be wrestling with the implications of the "touched" hand; he too was struggling to comprehend what being touched meant. It seemed to have evoked a trail of thought that brought him not so much to what it meant to be touched but to what it meant to be touched *there,* on *that* hand. Whether or not this was the first thing that had come to mind for him, his way of communicating his anxiety about my gesture was to "split off" the hand from the rest of his body, to excise the part that did the killing, as if the "trigger hand" had gone off on a killing rampage by itself. A well-known psychological concept that explains de Kock's language is "splitting." Splitting off parts of the self is a psychological mechanism that occurs at an unconscious level, but its effects are felt consciously, and help shift the gaze away from the individual's direct role in evil deeds: "That cannot be me. It was my 'trigger hand' that killed." Distancing himself from and casting away the evil part of his body was an effort at self-preservation. But it was also an illustration of how fragmented he was — a person broken into bits struggling to achieve some sense of wholeness.

De Kock's language was also a plea. He wanted me to reassure him that despite his murderous past, I would still be willing to reach out to him. He was exposed and alone in a country that, ironically, had employed mechanisms of denial to enable a regime of terror to thrive, and was now using denial to avoid facing responsibility for the past. *He* was not able to disown his past.

I was aware of a disintegration happening within myself. I was struggling with the part of me that made it possible to identify with de Kock — the evil de Kock. In a way, it was through "splitting" that I too was able to do this, for in my mind I had managed to separate the evil deeds from the doer, and could embrace the side of de Kock that showed some of the positive elements of being human.

De Kock's statement seemed to carry another underlying subtext as well. My action may well have been the first time a black person touched him out of compassion. He had previously met black people only as enemies, across the barrel of a gun or, for those who were on his side of the firing line, as comrades in murder. Perhaps de Kock recognized my touch as a kind of threshold crossing, a new experience for him. And he wasn't sure how to take it. Being touched placed him in a position of weakness, and drawing my attention to the power of the "trigger hand" was his way of reclaiming control over the situation. For the very act of drawing attention to the significance and the function of the "touched" hand that had killed innumerable blacks exalted it, confirming its status as the legendary Trigger Hand.

But what to do with a black woman's decision to break the skin barrier (and not only the skin barrier but also the moral barrier) and touch the Trigger Hand? In his uncertainty, his instinct was to put up new barriers in his mind. After all, who was this woman to offer consolation to the great de Kock, the grand architect who had laid waste to a million dreams? And so he returned to familiar ground: head of a covert operations unit, a crusader for apartheid, a strategist of mass violence. He was more comfortable seeing himself as an actor or initiator than as the object of another's compassion. That newer role, requiring him to be on the receiving end of human emotions, was somehow repugnant to his sense of how things should be.

I wondered about the ambivalence that the human contact between us seemed to have evoked in de Kock. Did he have trouble showing emotion in general, or was the confusion in him brought about by the question of my color? I had an advantage over him as far as the color issue was concerned, for in spite of apartheid, throughout my adulthood I have been surrounded by the richness of human diversity. For a significant part of my life, my relationships with people close to me and with acquaintances have crossed color lines, and my familiarity with and comfort in a multiracial world made it easy for me to sense discomfort in others who did not have a similar privilege.

"I don't see you as a black person," de Kock said when I asked him about the significance of race for him. He is not a racist, he claims, and justifies this assertion, as we've seen, by pointing out that his father grew up on a farm in the Eastern Cape and spoke three African languages, and that he, Eugene de Kock, had worked with blacks all of his life: "All my men were black " He obviously didn't think it significant that all of these relationships were with blacks who were his subordinates, and not just that but guerrillas who had been captured and turned to work for the apartheid cause.

De Kock's statement that he did not see me as black reminded me of a white student in my class at university more than ten years ago, where I was the only black in a group of six and he was the only man. This student had owned a farm in the conservative white part of the Western Cape, where the only blacks he had come into contact with were men he recruited from the homeland of Transkei and women who worked as maids in his house. In the first weeks of class he didn't seem to think that the rules of etiquette applied to his dealings with blacks. Nor did he have any concept of what cordial relationships with a black woman might look like. He couldn't engage in normal courteous conversation with me, such as asking, "How was your weekend?" So he related to me by trying to play peek-a-boo with me. When he walked past the small office where I often worked, the first thing he'd do was peek through my door, pretend to disappear, and peek again. I was of course amused by this grown-up man making a spectacle of himself as he tried to accommodate to me.

"I was one of the very few police, if not the only one, who did not have xenophobia," de Kock said. With some probing, he admitted that his relationship with black former guerrillas did not necessarily qualify as a basis on which to build normal and equal relationships with blacks. "One was not in a position then to talk to a person like you. If I met you ten years ago . . ." He let the sentence trail off, obviously realizing that he had put himself in a difficult position. "Ten years ago" he was deep in the heart of Vlakplaas, as its commander involved in cross-border "operations," executing or supervising murderous actions against blacks like me.

Images from de Kock's catalogue of unspeakable acts seemed to flood his mind, stopping him in his tracks as he tried to imagine what our encounter would have been like had we met ten years earlier. My own imagination was transported to that time of madness, and I thought about all those people whose paths had crossed his. Would I have considered meeting de Kock face-to-face ten years ago? It was hard to know.

It didn't matter. Watching de Kock struggling with his past was what mattered. It gave me a sense of hope that he was in some emotional pain about the things he had done. And the grace-filled gestures of forgiveness I had witnessed from people who lived with psychological scars as daily reminders of their trauma gave me even greater hope. In wrestling with my empathy, somehow I found solace in these gestures of forgiveness by victims. They validated my own feelings of empathy toward de Kock.

The first real turning point for me regarding my conflicting feelings toward de Kock came about five months after the trigger hand episode. At the First International Psychoanalytic Conference in Cape Town in April 1998, I presented for the first time a psychoanalytic interpretation of my interviews with de Kock. During the question period, a colleague asked whether I had considered the possibility that de Kock was "manipulating" me. I had expected that question and was well prepared for it. But before I could respond, Albie Sachs, a judge on South Africa's Constitutional Court, raised his arm — an arm that had been damaged by a bomb intended to kill him in Mozambique.[2] Instead of answering myself, I called on him. The packed room, filled with psychoanalysts from North America, the United Kingdom, and South Africa, grew hushed. Sachs spoke about how important it was "to see these men's humanity," and how much our hope as South Africans depended on reaching out to such glimpses of humanity in a spirit of compassion instead of revenge. Albie Sachs's words were all the more compelling because, as he spoke, he was gesturing with his cut-off arm.[3]

Much as some perpetrators might try to ask forgiveness, receiving it is unsettling for them. If they have hearts to feel remorse, how can their hearts allow them to forget? When de Kock uttered the words "ten years ago," he had opened a Pandora's box of memories, and he had to find a way to put the lid back on. What had started off as an examination of his attitude toward the race question had put him in a corner. After an uncomfortable pause he said, "But we were not open to that type of cultural mixing." He was clearly avoiding the word "race." "It was 'us and them,'" he said, summing up not only the prevailing racial attitude in South Africa under apartheid but also that between him and those he considered enemies. It was this level of distrust, deeply ingrained in his psyche, that made him uneasy and forced him instead to interrogate a gesture of warmth from a black woman's touch.

In the days and weeks after my rendezvous with de Kock in the TRC building, and during subsequent interviews with him at the prison, I kept going back to his comment about his trigger hand. As I tried to resolve my feelings about the statement, the act of touching him, and his responses to it, the idea of clear understanding became more and more elusive. Further conversations with de Kock made me believe, though, that the "trigger hand" statement was not intended to erect a boundary around himself. By touching the troubling murder "weapon," I had simply opened the floodgates of unwanted memory. In his cell, his past was a constant presence. "Look, you can do what you want, there is no way that you can erase it," he said about the ever-present images of death. "They may not be alive but they are there. They are there in the day, they are there in the morning. They are there at night when the sun sets. You can forget about forgetting — it's like a daily call card."

At the same time, his look of disbelief when I met him during a break in the TRC proceedings had a tinge of excitement: I had touched the untouchable part of him. My act of empathy had drawn me into intimate complicity with him. This too is possible. For the contradictions inherent in divergent interpretations of de Kock's "trigger hand" statement only tend to reinforce their validity. If evil is humanity turned against itself, then conflict and contradiction are fundamental to its nature. And if evil is in essence self-contradictory, then the interpretive conflicts engendered by his statement — the turmoil that seemed to burst from its surface — merely point to the urgency of de Kock's inner wrestling and the psychological instability inherent in the state of mind we call evil.

His terrors were real, for his trigger hand was still attached to his arm. He longed to be able one day to shed this cloak that burdened him, this intolerable shirt of flame, a first layer of which he said had begun to slip off with the commencement of the Truth Commission proceedings. Yet he also recognized that that day might never come, because in some ways the cloak was a part of him. Condemned and isolated under it, perhaps when I was drawn under its shadow for a brief moment of communion de Kock saw some hope. He longed to embrace the moment as proof that he was not alone in his universe, yet he didn't know how to do this. He was too diseased to grant himself that privilege. His world was a cold world, where eyes of death stared accusingly at him, a world littered with corpses and graves — graves of the unknown dead, dismembered or blown-up bodies. But for all the horrific singularity of his acts, de Kock was a desperate soul seeking to affirm to himself that he was still part of the human universe.

4

The Evolution of Evil

MY FOOTSTEPS ECHOED loudly off the walls as I walked the final long corridor leading to the room where I was going to meet de Kock. In the eerie silence of C-Max, interrupted only by the opening and shutting of the gates leading to my destination, I was suspended between memories of the sound of de Kock's voice during my last encounter with him on the ninth floor of the TRC offices and the cold feeling in my hand when I had touched his. I tried to rid myself of both memories. The guard jingled his large bunch of keys. We were approaching the last gate. I took a deep breath. "He is ready for you," said a second C-Max guard after examining the x-rayed contents of my bag on his computer screen.

De Kock was sitting in the same room where I'd conducted my first interview with him. Again he had chains around his ankles. He greeted me in the same fashion as he had the last time, rising and leaning against the wall to try and steady his shackled legs. Instead of the smile, he wore an embarrassed expression on his face as he extended his hand to greet me. "I'm sorry I didn't shave," he said, avoiding eye contact.

"They didn't tell me you were coming today. So I only had time to shower." On the day of our first interview, de Kock had looked as sharp as one might, considering the circumstances, dressed in his starched prison overalls, his face clean-shaven and hair well groomed. Today he looked a little unkempt.

"I'm really sorry for the way I look, Pumla," de Kock continued on the subject. I couldn't help the thought that there was something slightly contrived in his apologetic manner, as if it could have mattered to me that he convey the image of a perfect gentleman. I imagined the inner dialogue that may have played in his mind as he went through these motions. "After all, I am quite a decent guy. There are certain things one should just never do — like appearing unshaven before a lady." I couldn't help pondering the alarming irony of being concerned about rules of social etiquette when one has violated some of the most fundamental tenets of morality. Was it perhaps a way of reclaiming one's dignity, of holding on to some semblance of a belief in the decency of the self?

I looked at his hands for the first time, my eyes focusing on the left hand, the one I had touched, half expecting to see some peculiar features in it. But I did not. As if he was aware of my new interest in his hands, de Kock placed them squarely on the table to balance himself as he sat down. His fingernails were surprisingly neatly manicured. The nails were clean and white, with tidy symmetrical edges. One might even have been persuaded to call his hands beautiful. They could easily have been those of a friend or colleague. For a moment, it struck me that the line separating good from evil is paper-thin.

"He seems quite personable!" Leo Kamin, a friend whom I had taken to meet de Kock during one of the public hearings in

Cape Town, had remarked in amazement. Leo's wife, Marie-Claire, was equally baffled, hardly uttering a word as she shook de Kock's hand. She was still dumbfounded when I walked them back to their seats. "He looks like my brother!" Marie-Claire finally blurted out, her eyes still wide with bewilderment. It is this sense of a paper-thin line that is most frightening and most discomforting about those moments when our lives connect, however remotely, with the lives of people who have committed evil deeds. Could it perhaps also be a source of hope, that through our recognition of evil as a constant possibility in human experience we can learn to prevent it from taking over our lives?

As I sat down for my second meeting with de Kock, tape recorder, pen, and pad on the table, the question of de Kock's conscience was foremost in my mind. Had I been witnessing the reemergence of conscience? Was de Kock simply recreating his story for the benefit of present times? Where was his conscience when he returned again and again to murder those the apartheid government identified as its enemies? How does conscience get suppressed to the point where people can allow themselves to commit systematic acts of murder against others?

To begin to answer these questions, I knew I needed to take de Kock back to his very darkest hours. "What is your worst memory of the cross-border raids you conducted?" I asked him. "I have many," he said. "But one stands out in my mind more than the others." One morning he was driving home after a killing mission against the ANC's armed wing in a cross-border operation. He had done this many times. In fact, over the years he had lost count of how many people had died at his hands. But today seemed different. As he drove back from the killing field, he felt increasingly uncomfortable. He began to notice an odd smell on his body. At first, he dismissed it as the normal smell of discharged gunpowder, perhaps a little more caustic than usual but nothing particularly out of the ordinary. By the time he reached home at dawn, however, the acrid smell — now on his clothing as well — had become so unbearable that as he walked into his living room, he ripped his clothes off and threw them in a pile on the floor, then headed straight for the shower.

As he spoke, his facial muscles contorted; it was as if he were expressing revulsion at something he was reexperiencing even at that moment of retelling. He took a very long shower, he said, but it felt as if the pungent smell were still clinging to his body. "It was like the taste of metal in the mouth — the smell of blood all over my body. I couldn't get it off." His gestures had become extreme; he motioned in an exaggerated way, his eyes bulging, pulling at his arms as if he were struggling to remove something attacking his flesh, something undetachable from his skin.

Finally, he toweled off and waited. To no avail. The overpowering odor still clung. In all, he said, he ended up taking three or four more long showers, each time being careful to use a new towel. Unable to rid himself completely of the smell — the odor of death — he gathered the killing clothes into a plastic bag together with the first towel he had used and simply dumped them in the garbage bin.

It was a haunting story vividly told. In my mind it painted a clear picture of someone struggling with guilt, with a shadow that would not leave him and that he had tried to deny for too long. A human being died that night in the murder operation. This reality seemed to hang between us. At that moment I thought I saw a man finally acknowledging the debt he owed to his conscience.

*　　*　　*

It has often been said that most of the people who commit human rights abuses are not psychopaths, a psychological condition that is characterized by an inability to feel guilt. (A person whose conscience does not bother him may be "insane," according to the legal definition of psychopathy, with an inability to feel that makes it easy for him to repeatedly commit evil acts.) For a person who has a working conscience, who does extremely bad things even though his conscience tells him that what he is doing is wrong, explaining his behavior is complex. I have asked how conscience gets suppressed to the point where people can allow themselves to commit horrible acts against others. Should one ask as well what kind of society or ideology enables such suppression? Or is the question better illuminated by a consideration of group dynamics?[1] Was de Kock simply "caught up" in apartheid's grand plan of corruption?

The covert operations program did not "officially" exist but was clearly necessary for apartheid to survive. And to the extent that a bureaucrat like de Kock was able to maintain his two personae — his private self and his identity as apartheid's assassin — by buying into the ideology and mission of apartheid, he presumably could persuade himself that there was in fact something morally right about apartheid's covert program. But it was not just de Kock who bought into the ideology and corruption of apartheid. It was not just de Kock's conscience that was stilled. White society in general became numbed. The image of a deer frozen in the headlights of an oncoming car may resonate; a sense of being mesmerized and not being able to think clearly until the whole thing is over, and then wondering how one was able to behave in that way and did not speak out. Even the Afrikaans Church actively participated in providing justification for killing "enemies of the state." Army chaplains drove the message home through their sermons preached to soldiers of the South African army, who were issued a special copy of the Bible for easy reference to the inspirational passages.

There were two peculiar features that stood out about the Bible distributed to soldiers of the South African Defense Force. The first was the gold star-shaped army insignia embossed on the maroon front cover. The second was the inscription in Afrikaans on the first page, which read:

Message from the State President P. W. Botha

This Bible is an important part of your calling to duty. When you are overwhelmed with doubt, pain, or when you find yourself wavering, you must turn to this wonderful book for answers. . . . You are now called to play your part in defending our country. It is my prayer that this Bible will be your comfort so that you can fulfil your duty, and South Africa and her people will forever be proud of you. Of all the weapons you carry, this is the greatest because it is the Weapon of God.

Even this tampering with the book that many Christians consider sacred was not enough to provoke the condemnation it deserved from the church: the Afrikaans Church stood by silently and watched apartheid's murderous plan unfold.[2] This is the context in which de Kock's individual conscience took shape.

There were moments when it seemed that de Kock wanted to explore his past with me, to deepen his understanding of the levels to which he had been driven. I asked him how he saw his role under apartheid. "A crusader," he answered without hesitation.

"How did you become apartheid's crusader?" I asked him. "Did you choose the role yourself, or were you chosen because of certain qualities you possessed?"

"I've asked myself that question many times now," he said, looking gloomy, letting his voice trail off.

"Have you come up with any answers?"

"I want to understand. I mean, I know how it started. I can tell you about joining the army, Koevoet [the army's counter-insurgency unit, which de Kock led in Namibia], and all that. But your question — your question, the 'how,' I don't know. I don't know what to say." It was clear that this was an uncomfortable subject for him, and he was beginning to shift nervously. "I was not a security policeman long enough. I didn't have even a security police — I didn't even have the course. They didn't — I never even had a security police course, which they required of everybody before they can become a security police. I was effectively a cross-border machine and that is what they wanted. But I tell you. I see those faces today still. The shock, the fear, the desperation — the look of: This is it! I see those faces. Day — and night. They haunt. They haunt . . ." It seemed clear that de Kock understood the implications of my question as to whether he chose or was chosen.

To what extent was de Kock a normal, ordinary citizen corrupted by the apartheid system, and to what extent was his mind already corrupted by his own upbringing? When someone as part of his job must carry out orders that continually involve him in crimes against humanity, to what extent can he remain simply a person carrying out instructions, and at what point does evil intrude into and compromise the integrity of his conscience? How strongly does action — however mindless — reconstitute perspective, and perspective character? At what point did Eugene de Kock cross the moral line and take over — and upon himself, as a personal cause — the evil of the system for which he designated himself a crusader?

In my research and professional practice, I have time and again come across two fundamental positions — partly philosophical, partly empirical — regarding the nature and evolution of violence and personal evil. The first view holds that certain individuals are predisposed toward becoming evil as a result of early childhood experiences of violence that made them suffer shame and humiliation, leaving them with unresolved anger.[3] According to this view, the dynamics of evil that evolve from childhood psychological history often explain the roots of revenge, where anger and hatred resulting from the trauma suffered in the past are carried inside until the feelings of aggression can be enacted toward another in what becomes the individual's moment to reclaim the "honor" lost during the shaming experience.

De Kock's childhood was marked by emotional abuse at the hands of his father, whom de Kock has called "the proverbial hard man" and who drank too much.[4] Sometimes de Kock's mother was also a victim of her husband's wrath. De Kock described an incident in which he defended his mother when his father started attacking her with verbal slurs.[5] As a young boy, he had also suffered embarrassment and social shame among his peers because of a severe stuttering problem. He was clearly uncomfortable speaking at length about the distressing aspects of his childhood — an indication of the shame and embarrassment he still felt about it. "I have never forgotten the ridicule to which I was subjected," he told Jeremy Gordin in *A Long Night's Damage*.[6] Also, like many people who have suffered trauma in their lives, de Kock probably avoided talking about his early experiences because he had not fully engaged and integrated that part of his life. "There is still a lot of trauma there," he said, lowering his eyes and looking away. "There's a lot of trauma there."

So, one view of the evolution of evil would have it that what de Kock suffered at an early age established the basis for a life-long pattern of revenge-based behavior, but that his choice to become an aggressor did not authentically resolve the issues that drove that choice, or the feelings of shame and humiliation that lay within.[7] For de Kock, as for other violent perpetrators, violence does not confer what it promises; that is, what seemed at first to be a moment of honor reclaimed may draw itself out into a life of bondage to aggression as the person moves from one short-lived sense of honor regained to another. Each subsequent act lowers the threshold for committing the next by desensitizing the perpetrator, liberating him even further from society's taboos against aggression. The person may find aggression addicting not only because revisiting his unresolved feelings through violence brings temporary relief, but also because the repeated acts of aggression do not resolve the deeper feelings of being humiliated, disrespected, or dishonored. This plunges him once again into a spiral of violent behavior.

The second view on the issue maintains that evildoing is not the result of a predisposition, since most who have suffered unspeakable trauma do not turn out to be monsters. On this again partly philosophical, partly empirical view, people have free choice. The sovereignty of the heart is essentially inviolable. And though the decision to pursue what is right may on occasion be horrendously difficult, not only can people choose *not* to commit evil, but also they can make the kinds of choices that later on make it easier to avoid committing evil.

My own position is that the issue is more complex than ei-

ther of these two stances suggests. Those who have been traumatized *are* vulnerable to falling into a mode of psychological
repetition of the aggression they suffered.[8] Whether individuals turn out this way or that depends on a complicated set of
factors, one being whether they are "violently coached," another whether they are exposed to positive experiences that
can help mend the humiliation they suffered and restore their
sense of identity.[9] Those who do turn out to be violent are
more likely to have had direct or indirect encouragement to
be violent.[10] De Kock's given role, for example, as apartheid's
crusader indicates right away that he had a future of violence
carved out for him by national leaders. Should he have re-
sisted such forces as apartheid's legalization of violence and
the silent support by a society that benefited from the violence? Of course he should have. But could he have? Did he
have the conviction to oppose the system he served? Did
he have any of the unique resources that only the morally
courageous — the few who have the courage to follow their
conscience — possess in totalitarian societies? That one is
not confronted with the choices de Kock could have or could
not have made, that one was not a member of the privileged
class in apartheid South Africa are matters of sheer grace.
There is wisdom and insight in what Pulitzer Prize–winner
Tina Rosenberg says, that we "who interview and write and
judge, we are clear-eyed about the system's evil. . . . We know
how we would have behaved. It is [our] extreme good fortune
that we will never face this test."[11]

When, in addition to his own feelings of vulnerability, an individual is plunged into a system in which his career is defined by violence, then the issue of choice may not be as easy
as it seems. Violent abuse damages — and, yes, even corrupts
— the individual's psyche. It intrudes upon and invades the
victim's unconsciousness so that, in an environment that re-

wards evil, there are few resources on which the person can draw to resist it.

But this raises at least three sets of questions. If abuse only *damages* the person's psyche, is he like a person with an illness (hence someone who deserves society's sympathy)? Or if abuse also *corrupts* a person's psyche, does this imply that the person — through no fault of his own — will grow up predisposed to becoming a *morally* evil person? If the latter is the case — that abuse can predispose hitherto innocent people (children, or those working for an evil state) to evil — do they deserve our sympathy on the view that the corruption came from an external source and was imposed on them? Or do they deserve the same judgments we direct toward others who — however it came to pass — have become morally evil, not just people with a damaged psyche? And where is de Kock on this cognitive map? Is de Kock's culpability less? More?

Like sin, crime that is a gross violation of human rights almost always hides its true nature from its own self. It is by its very nature delusional: perpetrators of human rights violations redefine morality and start believing that they can commit systematic murder and other atrocities "for the greater good." The distance between evil and sickness is not that great. The evil component of crimes against humanity is the moral failing. The sickness aspect is the defect in perspective, the distortion in mental processing that both precedes the evil and is intensified by it. Foot soldiers like de Kock who are swept up by the ideology of evil regimes such as that of apartheid South Africa should be held morally responsible for the evil they commit. Their willingness to exercise their free will, to choose against the deepest parts of their conscience, should invite our condemnation.[12] But at the same time, some of them may need our sympathy, because under corrupt leadership they lacked appropriate models to steer them away from a violent path. Richard Rhodes, in his book *Why They Kill*, sketches out the interaction between violence and the experience of brutality. Criminal violence, he states, emerges from brutal social experience visited upon vulnerable children who return in vengeful wrath to plague society. Rhodes goes on to say, "If violence is a choice they make, and therefore their personal responsibility . . . our failure to protect them from having to confront such a choice is a choice *we* make."[13]

The sophistication and subtlety with which apartheid drew its followers to support its mission throw the idea of free choice into chaos. As shown earlier, apartheid turned religion on its head and, through various church-based structures in the military, the police, academia, and the church itself, provided a theological vocabulary to disguise the naked evil of what was being done. Chaplains who prayed that the "enemy" be defeated encouraged de Kock and many like him as forcefully as any covert coaching.

Yet when de Kock appeared at his 1995 trial, arrested by a post-apartheid government but in essence tried by the apparatus of the *former* apartheid state — the same Afrikaner judges, Afrikaner prosecutor, and Afrikaner state counsel — Anton Ackerman, the state attorney, set the scene for de Kock's trial by isolating him from the system that he had served. "This is not a political trial," Ackerman declared in an outrageous display of denial, a theme that came up repeatedly among lawmakers of the former apartheid state. De Kock's trial was about criminality. He was charged with "a heap of crimes that are universal: Thou shalt not kill; thou shalt not steal," Ackerman told the court.

Those who gave de Kock orders, who once worked hard to protect him from being found out, were no longer available or willing to go out on a limb for him. It was clear from the state attorney's opening remarks that the leaders of the old regime, among them apartheid's last president, Nobel laureate F. W. de Klerk, would stand at arm's length from de Kock's crimes — this despite the fact that de Kock had received many medals for his killing raids, including the highest national award for bravery, the Silver Star, and that his unit had been allocated millions in secret funds to establish its covert operations.

De Klerk, in a February 2001 address at Harvard University's Kennedy School of Government, defended his own moral distancing. In a "state of war," he said, foot soldiers in their zeal often go beyond what is legally acceptable and commit acts that are not authorized by the government. "The likes of Eugene de Kock," continued de Klerk in response to a question I asked him, should not have been allowed to apply for amnesty because of the gravity of their crimes. Asked whether he thought it was unreasonable for a man like de Kock to lay some of the blame on the president, de Klerk shot back, "My hands are clean."[14] Extraordinary, I thought, to encounter more hand imagery: de Klerk's pristine hands against de Kock's killing-machine one. Frustrated and rather saddened by what I saw as de Klerk's evasiveness in his dealing with my and others' questions about the past, I gathered my coat and bag and walked out.

One of the problems with trying individuals who have committed crimes under the explicit or implicit orders of their governments is that the law focuses strictly on the question of individual responsibility. All law does and must focus on individual responsibility because it is not possible to hold some "thing" responsible. It is the individual who must take the stand and be accused. But where the law fails in trying apartheid's — and so many other — human rights violations is that it focuses too heavily on particular individual crimes. The prosecutor in de Kock's case paid little or no attention to the question of structural and systemic crimes — the surrounding ideological/political philosophy, the setting up of Vlakplaas, and an administrative-executive system that protected and directed de Kock to commit the crimes for which he is now serving two life sentences. That the state attorney intended to frame de Kock's deeds as purely individual criminal acts was clear from his opening remarks.

Asked by the TRC whether they had authorized the crimes that were committed by apartheid's foot soldiers, the master architects of apartheid responded time and again that there was no official policy that supported illegal acts of violence. Yet when those who spoke out against apartheid were assassinated, died in police custody, or simply disappeared, when families in neighboring states who were thought to be harboring ANC members in exile were killed, when cars and buildings associated with the liberation movement exploded or burned down, no politicians called for an investigation into these "mysterious" occurrences. The proximate cause of these operations was the counterinsurgency unit. Yet although its role was not explicitly defined in any of the documents of the State Security Council (SSC),[15] the language of state violence — together with the intention — was clear. It pointed operatives like de Kock toward the destruction of "the state's enemies." And the state's enemies were those who fought to end apartheid and their supporters.

For years, apartheid politicians — and these, one should not forget, include apartheid's last president   did not regard the liberation aspirations of blacks with any seriousness. In the words of Justice Quartus de Wet, who sentenced Nelson Mandela to life imprisonment for sabotage, the regime's leaders were "not convinced" that Mandela and others were concerned about the human rights of all South Africans or about freeing blacks from the stranglehold of apartheid.[16] The liberation movement, they claimed, was a surrogate arm of the Soviet Union, a communist threat to "the democracies of the Western world," and not, of course, what it was: a threat to their own position of privilege and power. This made it easier for the most violent actions to be taken against the liberation movement; ostensibly, such violence was aimed not at the real citizens of South Africa but at a foreign enemy that had recruited blacks to its own purposes. In any case, blacks themselves, forced to carry passes to move around the country, were not considered South African citizens but something closer to foreigners in their own land.

In the context of the violence waged against "enemies of the state," Vlakplaas, the farm from which de Kock operated, became more clearly defined by the 1980s as the training ground of one of the units masterminding the state's violence against its political opponents. Yet de Klerk later dismissed de Kock and his colleagues as simply bad apples in a security department that was trying to cope with a war situation. De Kock had broken the boundaries of law in his overzealousness to execute instructions legally given to him, explained de Klerk.[17] This might have been more convincing if de Kock was the only apartheid operative who had "broken the law." Craig Williamson, the former security branch agent who was implicated in the murder of Ruth First and Jeanette Schoon and her six-year-old daughter Katryn,[18] had this to say about de Klerk's denial of knowledge of what was going on in his security forces: "All I can say is that if he believes what he says then his eyes were closed."[19]

The notion of a "misinterpretation" of instructions in the context of a covert operations unit appears intrinsically flawed. It seems that there is only one rule that governs covert political missions, and that is the rule of laissez-faire — having a free hand to do whatever it takes to achieve certain political goals. The fact that top-level members of government may not have ordered a particular act seems to be beside the point, since the instruction to do "whatever it takes" to get the job done has already been issued and, given that it is a *covert* operation, is the only instruction that will ever be issued. That purpose subsumes any particular decisions that the foot soldiers involved may take in carrying out their orders. For the highest echelons of South Africa's apartheid system to claim as a defense that they did not give specific orders for this killing or that bombing is as disingenuous as a defendant in a murder-for-hire plot claiming that he is innocent because he did not ask the assassin to use a .33-caliber shotgun — or even any shotgun — to kill his wife. He merely paid him to get her out of his way.

Not only that, but when de Kock and other operatives committed the kinds of crimes the government now says it never ordered, the government made no attempt to stop them or to investigate them afterward. When it did investigate, it was only after pressure from human rights organizations, progressive lawyers, and journalists. And even then, critical investigations into the crimes were often carried out by the same police officers who had been part of the covert operations in the first place.[20] Like many in his position, de Kock had immense freedom to fulfill apartheid's mission with the millions in secret funds the state pumped into his unit. Obeying the law was less important than being able to present some results to those in authority. The only concern was with what Craig Williamson called the "Eleventh Commandment": "Thou shalt not be found out."[21]

Apartheid's politicians differ fundamentally from leaders of criminal and genocidal regimes in other historical periods in the way they perceived the illegality of their actions and how they told their own story to themselves. Whereas other leaders embraced their government's criminal program and justified it to themselves by maintaining a belief in its rightness, South African leaders tried to distance themselves from the ugliness of apartheid violence by denying that it existed at all: the policy was to see no evil, hear no evil, speak no evil — and therefore admit no evil. Leaders like Slobodan Milosevic and Augusto Pinochet, for example, were deeply involved in the actions of their foot soldiers and often left a trail of direct orders connecting them to the crimes they masterminded. Similarly, at the end of World War II, sheaves of documents were found linking the actions of concentration camp overseers and other Nazi foot soldiers to direct orders from the top. In contrast, investigators in the post-apartheid era discovered, to their dismay, that the government's trail of blood ended right where the atrocities had been committed. It did not lead to the corridors of power. Was this only because apartheid's politicians were keen to avoid any future legal reprisals? Or was this careful demarcation of the political self from the sins of the nation also a psychological response to feelings of guilt over their own conduct?

Let's pause for a moment and consider the psychological coping mechanisms that those in authority in South Africa used to shield themselves from guilt, both legal and moral. State-sanctioned covert operations were first and foremost legally indefensible. Politicians knew this and were concerned to keep their hands clean, so to speak, by ensuring that there was no paper trail leading back to them. But there had to be *some* communication with those who would carry out the intentions of the state. Support for covert operations was therefore couched in ambiguous phrases that later enabled politicians to deny the real intent behind the words. Yet at the TRC hearings, documents were submitted into evidence suggesting that the mayhem unleashed by de Kock and his men was encouraged and expected, though not necessarily explicitly ordered, at the highest levels.

The papers sparked hot debate at the commission. Policy documents that had circulated at the State Security Council showed that expressions such as "making a plan," "taking out" enemy leaders, and "neutralizing," "eliminating," or "removing" certain people from society formed much of the lexicon of death within the upper levels of power. Although the documents were by any reasonable interpretation damning, explicit language that might have foisted clear accountability upon the leaders was carefully avoided, creating a gray zone of deniability that made it exceedingly difficult to determine the chain of command.

Yet to state assassins like de Kock, the same euphemistic verbiage that later provided a basis for de Klerk and his cabinet ministers to claim that their policies had been "misinterpreted" by zealots conveyed only one meaning: to snuff out those who stood in the way of the state. Brigadier Willem Schoon, a straight-talking soldier who at one point had been de Kock's immediate superior, made short shrift of the issue during his TRC hearings. "I don't want to be involved in semantics regarding the meaning of certain words in these documents," he said plainly. "I want to emphasize that words like 'eliminate' and 'to take out' for the members on the ground referred only to killing people." General Johan van der Merwe, a former commissioner of police, agreed: "Yes, definitely. If you tell a soldier to eliminate the enemy   he will understand that he has to kill."[22]

Referring to murder in euphemistic terms was, in one sense, merely an extension of the law of secrecy that formed the very basis on which the covert operations program was established. Top-level government officials used the need to keep the program secret to justify their use of secret language.

But in reality, what kept the program secret — although a South African would have had to be living in a cave not to know that it at least existed — was the relative lack of overt publicity about it.

Considering the lengths to which they went to erect this smokescreen of denial, it is possible that on some level South Africa's leaders did believe that they were doing nothing to encourage the killings. But the key portion of the apartheid belief structure was not that its leaders, like the members of Germany's Nazi Party, believed they were doing nothing wrong; there was too much counterevidence to maintain that with any degree of robustness. Rather, they believed that whatever they were doing wrong had to remain hidden from view, even from themselves. Killing apartheid's opponents became South Africa's dirty little family secret that everyone could see but no one openly talked about for fear that the house of cards called apartheid might come crashing down.

Comparing the statements of apartheid politicians to those of Nazis tried by the Nuremberg tribunal raises questions about the issue of moral, as opposed to legal, guilt and innocence. The Nazis never denied involvement in what they had ordered, supported, or encouraged. What they denied was that it was criminal. By contrast, apartheid politicians, once stripped of power and exposed to the logic of international and domestic law, never denied that killing and torturing liberation activists was criminal. What they denied was that they were ever involved in it or knew anything about it.

What does this say about the question of conscience in the two cases? Which leadership type betrays the greater level of depravity? Is the politician who plunges openly into criminal behavior and, Nazi-style, shamelessly denies there is anything wrong with it more or less morally degenerate than one who lies about his criminal behavior to cover it up? In the great biblical story of the Fall, would tradition have judged the first humans as more innocent or more brazen if, rather than running away to hide after their sin, they had walked up to God and looked him directly in the face? Does knowing that you are wrong and persisting in it reveal a greater depth of moral decadence (or psychic damage) than having the kind of malfunctioning ethical compass that makes you unable even to realize *that* you are wrong? Which kind of individual is the more redeemable?

It is difficult to comment on the question of conscience in apartheid leaders because it was never raised with those who were summoned before the TRC. In her book *Eichmann in Jerusalem*, Hannah Arendt analyzes Adolf Eichmann's tribunal testimony after the Auschwitz concentration camp commander was captured by Israeli secret police in an attempt to unearth the sources of Eichmann's capacity to do what he had done. Arendt wants "to know how long it takes an average person to overcome his innate repugnance toward crime, and what exactly happens to him once he has reached that point."[23] Her task is a formidable one, because she is trying to reach deep conclusions about a perpetrator's inner motivations on the basis only of reading written testimony and listening to oral testimony during Eichmann's trial. She did not have a chance to question him. Nevertheless, Arendt is able to conclude that Eichmann did have a conscience, "within rather odd limits."[24] And if Eichmann had a conscience, as Arendt claims, then this suggests that he was not a sadistic individual psychologically "programmed" to engage in mass killings, but rather that he had contemplated, perhaps even struggled over, what he was doing.

I find it difficult to see the evidence that Eichmann had a working conscience. In his book *Eichmann in My Hands*, Peter Malkin, who captured Eichmann on the streets of Buenos

Aires, talks about his frustration in trying to discover some element of humaneness in Eichmann during the hours he spent guarding him after his capture and before he was flown to Israel for his trial. In an attempt to make Eichmann relate to the human loss he had caused, Malkin told him about his sister's son, with whom he was very close, and how he was taken away to be killed in Auschwitz. Eichmann, looking "genuinely perplexed," as if Malkin had said something wrong, responded, "But he was Jewish, wasn't he?"[25]

Yet Malkin reports that while Eichmann expressed no pangs of conscience, and he found little or no trace of humaneness in Eichmann, he himself was changed by the conversations with him:

> [T]hose sessions caused me to reflect on my own actions in ways I never had before. I realized that in the course of my career I had participated in actions that were unjust, perhaps even criminal. Always I had followed my superiors' orders absolutely, most of the time for what seemed noble reasons . . . yet also because it was also a matter of habit. I would never be that easy on myself again, or find excuses to deny the hard evidence of my eyes, and ears, and heart. For the fact is as simple as it is inescapable: If the conscience stops functioning, even occasionally, one is in mortal danger of losing oneself.[26]

Eichmann saw neither moral nor legal wrong in the genocidal killings that he summed up with this "explanation": They were Jews. This underscores an element that was absent from apartheid's policy of murder, and perhaps points to different ways of understanding conscience in the Nazi and apartheid cases. The Nazi conscience was so warped that it had become a clear conscience. One might say without too much exaggeration that the apartheid conscience, by contrast, was so ridden with guilt that it had to be circumvented. Unlike hatred of the Jews, who were regarded by the Nazis as vermin, the "scum of the earth," the hatred of blacks by the Afrikaners, at least at the policy level, did not reach the proportions that allowed the Nazis to formulate the Final Solution.[27] The South African leadership may have wanted to create separate societies, but their policies do not reflect a felt need for a cleansing of society, or for the extermination of one group by another as in other examples of state-orchestrated brutality.

How can we understand these cultural differences between violent societies? If, in one case, as with the Nazis, there seems to have been no threshold for tolerance of the extermination of Jews, and in the apartheid case there seems to have been some threshold, to the extent that those in authority wanted to remain at moral arm's length from what was done in their name, how can the different forces that operate in these violent societies be explained? Are there psychological, social, or religious reasons that can help clarify why apartheid politicians seemed so concerned about image? It appears that there were certain checks at the very time these atrocities were taking place, an awareness both in private and in public of a moral wrong being committed. This certainly created a contradiction, since the silence of politicians clearly served to support the wrong that was being done. In Germany, Nazi ideology and the idealization of the Aryan self seem to have produced a belief that the leaders were in a sense above morality, that they were involved in a grand scheme to which ordinary criteria for judging what is moral did not apply. In fact, Nazis had to renounce their religious faith and pledge allegiance to Hitler as if he were above God.[28] Apartheid politicians, by contrast, were ardent followers of the Christian faith. *All* apartheid presidents except F. W. de Klerk belonged to the Afrikaans Church, that is, the Dutch Reformed Church. De Klerk's church was a different denomination of the same order of faith, the Reformed Church (Gereformeerde Kerk).

In 1981 Eugene de Kock was based in Oshakati, Namibia, where he led the notorious counterinsurgency unit of the South African army, the Koevoet. In de Kock's camp morning services were conducted in different languages to accommodate the black Angolan and Namibian members of de Kock's unit. "One day we would read the Afrikaans Bible, then the next day the Ovambo Bible, then the Portuguese Bible, because half of my troop were Portuguese-speaking. The other group were Ovambo Bushmen, you know," de Kock said. One morning the sermon was based on a reading from the Book of Psalms: "He is the God who avenges me, who subdues nations under me, who saves me from my enemies."[29] The chaplain, who has since died in an accident, but whose name de Kock didn't want to mention ("to protect his family"), had prayed during the service that God would deliver the enemy into the soldiers' hands, into the hands of "God's army."

On any given day when de Kock and his troop went into the bush, they could predict where and when they would find guerrillas of the liberation army of the South West African People's Organization (SWAPO). This morning they thought they would have an easy time. "It was a quiet day, and we were not expecting to fight, really; we were just — lackadaisical-like," de Kock said. But on their way to Okanjara, four SWAPO guerrillas jumped out unexpectedly from a bush in front of de Kock and his men. Three guerrillas were killed, and the fourth one captured.

The knapsacks of the killed and captured guerrillas were searched. Often these searches yielded the usual army equipment. On this occasion, however, de Kock was surprised to find a Bible. Its pages were quite worn. "I looked at this, and it was well paged. I mean you could see — it was not neglected. It was read regularly," he said.

"You were surprised?" I asked.

"Here we have a SWAPO man who is supposed to be a communist, who is supposed to be the enemy, the personification of the Antichrist, who also ten-to-one that morning may have read the same Scripture lesson that said the enemy will be given into your hands. Now, on whose side is God now? Even today still I sit and — I expected to find a Little Red Book there or one of Lenin's condensed writings. And here they had the same Bible that my men and I carried in our rucksacks. They've got exactly the same Bible . . ." De Kock's voice trailed off and he looked somewhat startled, as if the incident were as fresh as it had been sixteen years earlier.

It was hard to believe that de Kock found anything remarkable about finding a Bible in an "enemy's" bag. Wars have been fought in which both sides shared the same faith. Why should this have such an impact on de Kock? I wondered if at the time he found himself faced with a moral dilemma. Or if the problem was simply that the discovery cut off the head of the very justification de Kock needed to maintain his destructive zeal.

"I started reflecting on the war, on the way it was presented, and asking myself a lot of questions," he said.

"What was the nature of your reflection? Did it alter the way you thought about this war with so-called communists?" I asked him. "Did you *do* anything?"

"Well, no. But you come across something like that in the middle of the bush, you start asking yourself questions, and your conviction starts wavering. Since then, there were many times I felt like this," de Kock said.

The idea of de Kock's conviction "wavering" in 1981,

though he still went on to amass a legendary record throughout the 1980s as head of death squad operations in the security
police, sounded a little spurious.[30]

De Kock's internal torment, manifested in the incident of
the smell that wouldn't wash off, was largely an unconscious
process, the deeper roots of which were perhaps too hidden
from consciousness to lead to any reflection and to effect any
real change. But this other incident of the Bible was right
there before his eyes, if not as proof, at least as enough evidence for him to question the justification of the war as a mission against the Antichrist.

How much evidence is necessary for one to change perspective and for transformation in one's life to result? Is knowledge enough to change a person's heart? Is it sufficient simply
to know that the beliefs on which one has based one's behavior are wrong? Perhaps one doesn't need more knowledge; one
needs the resolve to use the knowledge that one has. Moving
from reflection to engagement requires a new way of seeing
the old — the kind of shift in perspective that information
rarely yields but spiritual conviction sometimes brings.[31]

In neither teaching nor example did the army's spiritual
leaders, the chaplains, create a moral climate in which the soldiers could draw from their religious convictions and exercise moral restraint. The unimaginable horrors committed
by de Kock's Koevoet unit were perpetrated not only as part of
a broad political and military strategy to destroy SWAPO and
its supporters and to terrorize ANC sympathizers, but also as
divinely sanctioned acts. Thus, the government interpreted
all religious objections to the war as inconsistent with spiritual conviction. Soldiers who refused to participate in apartheid's war on the grounds of conscientious objection were
severely punished.[32] P. W. Botha believed that reporting for
military duty was answering God's call to fight the Antichrist.

"The honor and duty to defend one's country shouldn't be made subservient to one's religious convictions," he said.[33]

"Tell me about this — *wavering*," I asked de Kock. "I'm trying to understand how you could have continued for so long fighting in the bush and then returned to South Africa to run Vlakplaas if you had serious questions about apartheid's mission."

"No, I did," de Kock said defensively. "But look, I was truly, or I had no, and absolutely no reason to believe that we are going to have a different situation in South Africa than we had in the Congo in the sixties.[34] There was nothing that pointed me in a different light; whether it was naive or uninformed I don't know. I myself have kept abreast as much as possible of what happened in the rest of Africa. And all indications were that South Africa would go the way of the rest of Africa if the ANC took over. And we had to protect the country from this. The overall and general hue and cry was 'Fight, resist, sacrifice, or you will be wiped out by the black man.' Rule by the black man was a sure means of destruction of the country."

"But your killing operations were *causing* destruction "

"I am trying to establish things myself," de Kock said with some agitation before I could finish, "and it's still very difficult —"

"Well, *I'm* trying to establish what you mean when you say you had doubts, that you started asking yourself some questions, that your conviction wavered, and yet you stayed on. There is no indication that you brought what you were doing to a stop, even for a month, a week, a short while, just to seriously reconsider your involvement in these killing operations. I want to understand why."

"Even after I came back from Namibia to work at Vlakplaas, I did; there were those times when I just — you know, you would just stop and think about where things were going. Well, on the one hand, you thought about what would happen to you if things turned around, if the other side won. But sometimes you started to mull these things over in your head. Inherently you know that killing is not right. The killing has been sanctioned by the highest authority. But then you have to be on this particular mission because the ANC killed some of your own people. A bomb planted by the military wing of the ANC at the Wimpy Bar killed children, women — families. Then the heat goes up. People — in government and white society — start asking what we are doing for the security of the country. Everybody in the security looks for targets, people responsible for the bomb, you know. One thing I would like to bring to your attention is that there were correspondence and telephone calls to C1, Vlakplaas, by applicants. Each and every one, from officers to lower ranks, wanted to fight terrorism. Every time the ANC hit targets — civilians — the number of requests to join Vlakplaas went up. There was anger on our side, and people wanted to stop the other side. So, we get our targets. Then there's retaliation. As I said, the crucial thing was to get the job done. The question of whether what we did was legal or not did not come into the picture. How we did it was not important. The results were. People wanted to see results. They wanted to know that we were rooting out what at the time we called terrorism."[35]

Evil was done in the name of apartheid. De Kock's actions were part of a long-standing policy of using terror as a weapon against opponents of the state. But it is hard to see where direct responsibility for such evil lies. In a high-pressure crisis system like that of South African apartheid, where lines of responsibility begin to clash and fuse together into a confusing stew, you cannot put your finger on the one "true" source of responsibility. When responsibility is shared, it makes it that much harder for any one individual to assume his or her part.[36]

It made me wonder if a similar dynamic may have existed between the young black activists who killed suspected black police collaborators from their own communities with a burning tire around their necks — the brutal "necklace" killings — and their leaders in the mass democratic movement that emerged in the 1980s. And if I let off the black necklace murderers in my mind, would intellectual honesty force me to let off the likes of de Kock as well? In relation to the necklace murders, were black people who were bystanders to these gruesome human burnings really in a similar situation to that of the South African white community, who chose to believe official reports in the newspapers about the war that South Africa was fighting? Are the roles of perpetrator, victim, and bystander so mutually interchangeable?

"We failed our children," said one woman during interviews I was conducting in Mlungisi, an Eastern Cape township once devastated by apartheid's war and by necklace murders. "We failed to protect them, not just those who were burnt by the necklace, but those who did this terrible thing. We sat here and watched. We did or said nothing. The whole community. We sat here hoping somebody will do something to break this cycle of insanity. It has left us with this terrible unhealable scar, knowing that we could have, but we didn't."

Could have, should have, didn't — it was all very complicated. In the fluidly unfolding events of a necklace murder, was there time and space to stop the killing? And in a community of people depressed by their circumstances, beset by life's struggles, thwarted in their hopes, how do you bring such an act into the range of possible choices? How do you even make it thinkable?

Was there space and time for de Kock to stop *his* carnage?

"Something envelops you during that action time," de Kock said. "There you are — like, become automatic," he said. "Then the training takes over: Everything is, like, automatic. But afterwards it is like — it is like you are — well, I personally was totally, totally drained, mentally but even physically. When you are psyched up, or hyped up, your training takes over, and also your fear."

It was interesting to listen to him struggle to find the words to construct what turned out to be unreconstructible, experiences that defied comparison.

"Fear?" I asked.[37] "Were you afraid of the people you targeted in your operations? Did you see them as people?"

"Well, yes. There were times I was afraid; you could get killed yourself. And I did see them as people.[38]

"In that second or two seconds, you are on automatic because your training takes over. You don't allow yourself to think of the faces you see. The moment you pulled the trigger you were already going to the next target. It's very very fast, in a way surgical. Cold. You are in an emotional block, or else you wouldn't be able to pull the trigger. The fear, it's like an aura surrounding you. You cross the border and enter the surreal. Your heart is going about 200 at that stage. Everything becomes a sort of a blur, but you have to move."

This element of the surreal conjures up images of fantasy, something happening outside the boundaries of reality — a perception of one's victims as less real, less present as human beings, than they were. De Kock might have experienced *himself* as less real, as if he and his victims were floating in a trance or as if in a motion picture. In fact, de Kock used motion picture imagery to describe how one of his victims, Zwelibanzi Nyanda, was killed in a cross-border operation de Kock masterminded. KwaZulu/Natal security policemen in Ermelo and in Piet Retief had targeted Nyanda, a leader in the

ANC's military in Swaziland, for killing. De Kock described how he shot Nyanda as he was running away from gunfire. "Zwelibanzi Nyanda came through that window from the bathroom," said de Kock. "It was — just like somebody burst at you. I was outside. It was not like he was struggling to get out of the window. I mean, he was virtually exploding from it. It's weird. You would have to get someone who knows about aftereffects — no, not 'aftereffects.' You know, like they have in the movies — 'special effects.' To reconstruct something like that, it would need someone who knows something about special effects."

Robert Lifton, in his book *The Nazi Doctors*, argues effectively that in order for the Nazi "medical" experiment to be successful, doctors in Auschwitz had to relate to their environment as if it were some kind of fantasy and not part of the real world.[39] There was an absence of awareness, not only of one's surroundings but also of oneself. To make it work over and over again, this psychological cutting off of one's sense of reality needed constant justification.

"At that stage, everybody was looking to the north [of Africa] and saw what happened in what is now the Democratic Republic of Congo," de Kock said again, "and saw how all of that was brought down, and repeated closer to home in the neighboring states. This is why we had to fight in these countries [Zimbabwe, Namibia, Angola, Mozambique] as well, to stop the threat of communism, especially when they [the "enemy" countries] became friendly with the ANC. But now, at the end of the day, I realize that I am actually a veteran of lost ideologies. I fought in Rhodesia; I saw action in Angola, South-West Africa [Namibia] — in basically all the neighboring states — and then here [in South Africa]."

"How do you feel, being a victim of lost ideologies?" I asked.

"I think that I lost — it's a feeling of loss. Well, the first thing that goes is innocence, I mean, there's no more fairy tales and Bambi. That is gone. We killed a lot of people, they killed some of ours. We fought for nothing, we fought each other basically eventually for nothing. We could have all been alive having a beer. And the politicians? If we could put all politicians in the front lines with their families, and grandparents, and grandchildren — if they are in the front line, I don't think we will ever have a war again. I think it's educated people, very educated people, who sit in parliament and decide about war. So I am confused, I am very confused, I am just very tired." De Kock shook his head, shifted his legs to adjust the position of the chains that bound him to his seat, his eyes downcast, looking like somebody reflecting on the greatest loss in his life.

5 ⇓

The Language of Trauma

TO EXPERIENCE EMPATHY for someone who has committed terrible acts against other human beings, as I did with Eugene de Kock, puts one in a strangely compelling and confusing relationship with the perpetrator. Especially when, as is the case with me, my experience while a member of the TRC centered on victims and placed me in powerfully empathic relationships with them. I became especially concerned with how victims of politically motivated violence live with traumatic memory, and how this shapes their narratives about events. It is this focus on victims — on victims' memory and language of violent trauma, on the intimate, fraught relationship between victim and perpetrator, and on victims' extraordinary power to forgive — that I wish to return to in this chapter.

The Truth and Reconciliation Commission was established in December 1995 after the appointment of seventeen commissioners by then-president Nelson Mandela.[1] Archbishop Desmond Tutu was appointed to serve as the chairman of the Truth Commission. There was probably no one more suited to the role of chairman for the historic process of the TRC than Archbishop Tutu. He is an extraordinary man whose dignity and stature, both in South Africa and internationally, and whose pursuit of peace and justice earned him the Nobel Peace Prize in 1984. He carried his role on the TRC with grace both in public and in those moments behind closed doors when suspicion and racial tensions among TRC members emerged, signaling the ever-present struggle with identity politics in a country where for so many years race, more than anything else, determined who a person was.

The commission added ten more committee members in 1996 to work with the commissioners, and I was appointed one of them. A central part of my work as a clinical psychologist had included providing expert testimony for human rights lawyers who were defending young anti-apartheid activists charged with serious crimes. The invitation to join the TRC was particularly significant for me because my role as an expert witness had given me an opportunity to see firsthand how the hostility of apartheid courts often deprived blacks, both victims and defendants, of a fair hearing. It gave me a great sense of purpose to be invited to join a process uniquely designed as a forum where victims could break their silence and face their abusers for the first time. I was privileged to serve as the only trained psychologist on the Human Rights Violations Committee at the head office of the TRC in Cape Town, and later to be appointed coordinator of the victims' public hearings process in the Western Cape region, with responsibilities that included community outreach, identifying areas where public hearings could be held, supervision of the statement-taking and hearings processes, and chairing public hearings in the Cape Peninsula and winelands regions.

One of the first things I did when I joined the TRC in March 1996 was to submit a proposal for an outreach program at one of the Cape Town office's weekly regional meetings. The first public hearings of the TRC were scheduled to take place a month later in East London. My proposal was for a program designed to be an informational process — not a formal hearing — that would reach out to all levels of society and all racial groups.

The Cape Town office launched the TRC outreach program in the Gugulethu Township of Cape Town with the help of Mandisa Monakali, director of a counseling agency for women victims of domestic abuse, and Miriam Moleleki, director of an organization that brings together children and families from diverse racial backgrounds in the Worcester township, Zwelethemba. Mandisa Monakali also worked with women who had been raped while in detention or by members of political organizations in conflict with one another. Monakali, her staff, and Miriam Moleleki, who had won several awards for her dedication to rural development, played a crucial role in getting the TRC office started on its initial outreach work in the black townships around Cape Town.

The first outreach meeting we organized was held in a small hall in Gugulethu Township. The room was overflowing. The only white people present were TRC members and reporters, some of whom had come to cover the event, and others who simply wanted to return to the place of their troubled days of reporting political violence under stringent apartheid press laws. We had asked Archbishop Tutu to preside over the meeting. It was clear from the way people attending the meeting greeted Tutu that his leadership of the TRC and his presence, whether actual or symbolic, was going to be a vital part of the commission's work. For people burdened with the memory of a traumatic past, Archbishop Tutu's presence validated the pain they had suffered.

What was most amazing about the meeting in Gugulethu

was the intensity of opposing emotions expressed in the hall. There was a spirit of celebration in evidence in the singing and dancing in which everybody joined, as if bound together in shared expectations for the future and by the freedom that the TRC process promised — the freedom to speak out and to break the years of silence. At the same time, many in the audience had both a sense of painful anticipation and a desire to make sense of the scale and scope of what had happened to them and their loved ones.

The people started to speak one by one. But the audience was not a coherent whole, for each member of it had lived through pain differently. One person after another got up to testify in an outpouring of emotion: this one about her son, whose death at the hands of the police she lacked appropriate words to describe and for whom a stream of tears was the only thing that could communicate her deep sorrow; that one about losing his eyesight after a policeman nicknamed "the Rambo of the Western Cape" pointed his firearm directly at his eyes and fired; and another about searching for his son, first at police stations, and then in mortuaries, including the Cape Town government mortuary, where he had to open many drawers holding dead bodies, most of them bloody, brutalized, and dismembered, and to step over other bodies in one room after another before finding his son in a dark corner on a shelf packed with corpses. The testimonies were hard to take in, and one couldn't help wondering: if the experience was emotionally heavy for us, the listeners, how much more so must it be for the people for whom the trauma was embedded in their identity? I was paralyzed. It took me some time to remember that this was meant only as an initial gathering, not a public hearing of the TRC. No matter; the victims were seizing the moment to break the silence imposed on them for so long, as if there were an uncontrollable pressure to tell their stories.

I became aware of the desperate need for such a process soon after appearing on a radio program in which the TRC's outreach program in the Western Cape was discussed. I had mentioned Mandisa Monakali's agency in Gugulethu Township as one that would help the TRC in gathering statements. As soon as I got home, the telephone rang. It was Monakali.

"There is an elderly lady here in my office who wants to speak to someone from the TRC," Monakali said. "And Pumla," Monakali said with some urgency, "you have to come."

I was soon on the freeway to Gugulethu. When I arrived at the agency an elderly woman, Mrs. Elsie Gishi, was sitting on a couch, leaning forward on her walking stick, her eyes fixed on the door. She had walked for about thirty minutes to the agency, accompanied by a young boy, a teenager from her neighborhood. She rushed through the greetings and started to tell her story. Mrs. Gishi began with her arrival in Cape Town with her husband as a young bride, then told of her work as a domestic in different homes in the white suburbs of Cape Town, her hardworking husband, the joy of raising their children, their schooling, and finally the events of that fatal Christmas Eve in 1976 when her husband was killed.

In the months following the events of June 16, 1976, when the police massacred more than five hundred people in Soweto, violence had flared up in many black townships. The government stepped up its repressive measures, leading to thousands of deaths. By the end of the year, many families and communities had been affected by the state's violence, and Christmas that year was declared a "Black Christmas." It was the events of the Black Christmas in the Cape Town township of Nyanga East and the informal settlement referred to as KTC that Mrs. Gishi described, using images of her neighborhood as a war zone: army trucks roaming the streets, gunfire reverberating menacingly throughout the township, black men who were police collaborators carrying homemade weapons and charging from house to house, looking for male members of the households like hunters cornering their prey.

Mrs. Gishi described her state of panic on a day she recalled as "bright, with a clear sky," as she roamed the streets looking for her children in the midst of wild firing. She was finally forced to flee the streets but was hit by bullets in her back just as she entered her neighbor's house. Injured, frightened, and helpless, she landed in the hospital, where she was chained to her bed and placed under police guard, as was common practice with many victims shot by the police in incidents of a political nature.[2] While in the hospital she was told by neighbors that her husband had been found dead in their home, his head slashed open, exposing his brain. Mrs. Gishi came home from the hospital to find that she had suffered a double loss. Her son had gone mad: "One of my neighbors told me that my son was in the same van in which my husband was taken to hospital. What my neighbor described to me broke my heart completely. My son — my son Bonisile insisted on accompanying the wounded to the hospital. So he was in the back of the van and saw his father in the worst and most unspeakable state of death any child should see. I was told that he repeatedly asked his dead father, '*Tata, Tata* [Daddy], do you see me, do you see me? Please say yes to me.' He was crying and shaking my husband. On my return from the hospital I found my son's bloodied clothes from throwing himself all over my husband's body. . . . [S]ince then my son has not been his normal self."

It was hard not to be drawn into her story. I saw this little boy's agony, his tears of anguish and utter hopelessness as he stared into the unseeing eyes of death, knowing but not knowing — "*Tata*, please say yes to me" — that his father wouldn't be able to speak to him again.

My thoughts came back to this seventy-two-year-old woman seated before me, the indelible mark left by the traumatic event returning like a flash when she heard about the TRC over the radio, twenty years after her trauma, recalling the event with overwhelming urgency.

Her story seemed to present the sense of before and after so vividly, the shift from one moment to the next that changes everything: a normal and happy life interrupted by the events of that Black Christmas of 1976; a bright day and a clear blue sky ruined by rampant slaughter; her son, one moment a happy, normal child, the next a boy who has lost his sanity. There was something bizarre about the images she presented, something bordering on the obscene — something beyond words. She described what had happened to her husband and what her son had seen as a "most unspeakable state of death." In other words, it was simply *indescribable*. She had no reference point against which to relate the experience. She was doing what many victims and survivors of trauma have done, which is to frame their testimonies in language that they themselves find inadequate to describe their experiences.[3]

And here lies the paradox. Language communicates. At the same time, it distances us from the traumatic event as it was experienced, limiting our participation in the act of remembering. We cannot fully understand what victims went through, in part because the impact of the traumatic event cannot be adequately captured in words. So what function does a victim's testimony serve if it only creates a gulf between language and experience?[4] Is its function to force us to see the real story of a violent political past? Is its aim to direct us to the *real* story behind traumatic memory, which is embedded in the emotional scars carried by thousands of victims and survivors who reflect daily on the destruction visited upon their lives by a brutal political system? It is a story that will always be true for the victim, for the victim is exposed to the images of the trauma through memory. The "facts" of the traumatic experience are written on the victim's body and heart and remain an indelible image of what the victim suffered.

When the rupture of one's senses is a daily occurrence, as in South Africa's violent political past, old memories fuse with new ones. The narratives of trauma told by victims and survivors are not simply about facts. They are primarily about the impact of those facts on victims' lives and about the painful continuities created by the violence in their lives. There is no closure.[5] The lived experience of traumatic memory becomes a touchstone for reality,[6] and it tells us more than facts can about how people try to lead a normal life after such a trauma.

Traumatic memory renders the account of past events unreliable, or so the argument goes. Primo Levi tells us that "[h]uman memory is a marvelous but deceptive tool."[7] What lies in our memory is not engraved in stone but fades away with time, shifts or swells. This argument has led many to question victims' stories and to claim that what is remembered amounts to fragments of fact, a reconstruction of past events, and fails to rise to the level of truth. Some argue that the memory of traumatic events necessarily involves forgetting.[8] While these claims are not unfounded, they implicitly suggest that remembered traumatic events have an element of unbelievability. But do *factual* accounts of traumatic events tell us how victims have lived and continue to live with the memory of their trauma? As we on the commission listened to the accounts of victims and survivors who appeared before us over hours, days, weeks, and months, their narratives brought into focus the painful, daily invasion of traumatic memory in their lives. It seemed that rather than a *recon-struction* of their traumatic past, what victims and survivors brought to the public hearings of the TRC was their lived experience of traumatic memory. Could the reason for Mrs. Gishi's urgency to tell her story be the indelible *presence* of the trauma she had suffered twenty years before?

Not all victims experienced the same sense of urgency that Mrs. Gishi's story illustrates. Some believed that they had laid their trauma to rest, and were afraid that if they spoke out about it, they would be opening up a torrent of emotions that they would not be able to control. But even when victims seemed to recoil from the TRC process, when they told their stories they did so with the same level of intensity as other victims who approached the TRC with a feeling of urgency.

I am reminded of a woman, Mrs. Plaatjie, whose eleven-year-old son was killed by the police in Queenstown in the township of Mlungisi in 1986. Mrs. Plaatjie had walked out during a TRC outreach meeting that I had organized with the head of the Investigative Unit of the TRC, Dumisa Ntsebeza. Ntsebeza was addressing the audience when I noticed a woman sitting defiantly with her back to the stage. I immediately understood the body language and went to speak to her. As I was approaching, she turned away from me, got up from her seat, and started to walk out. I followed her, and I could hear her speaking, at first softly as if to herself, and then directly to me: "Why did you come here? Why did you come here?" Some in the audience turned to look as I followed her out. When we got outside, she began to cry, and continued tearfully: "Have you come here to hurt us? Just tell me, have you come here to open our scars?" She continued to speak through a mixture of tears and anger. The TRC was "a pointless exercise," she said. She had forgotten her pain, she told me, and had "put grass over the past," using a Xhosa expression, the main language of the Eastern and Western Cape. "And now you want us to remember? Is this going to bring back my son?" Mrs. Plaatjie asked tearfully.

We sat under a tree, and I noted her quiet pain as she wiped her face and tried to regain her composure. I was lost for words and felt helpless with guilt for the hurt that our outreach presentation had evoked. I offered to take her home, and as we drove to her house, I felt like a messenger who travels around villages bringing bad news, breaking people's hearts, without staying to pick up the pieces.

Mrs. Plaatjie invited me into her modest two-room home — in the front room two chairs, a table, and a cupboard, and in the other, smaller room a twin bed. She pointed me to a chair and sat in another one facing the only window in the room, her eyes contemplative but sorrowful as the afternoon sun shone on her face. Then she began to tell her story.

"My son was eleven. He came home during school break at ten o'clock. I was sitting right there where you are sitting, just sitting exactly where you are sitting in that chair. He walked in dressed in his school uniform and went to the cupboard over there and cut himself a slice of bread. He is doing all of this in a rush. He is like that when he comes home during break. He spread peanut butter on it and then put the rest of the bread back, leaving the crumbs all over the cupboard, and the knife, still smudged with peanut butter. He ran out. He is still chewing his bread and holding it in his hand. It wasn't long — I heard shots outside. Some commotion and shouts. Then I'm hearing, 'uThemba, uThemba, nank'uThemba bamdubule! [This is Themba. They have shot Themba!]' and then someone calling out for me: 'mama kaThemba! [Themba's mother!].' I went flying out of this house. Now I am dazed. I ran, not thinking. My eyes are on the crowd that has gathered. Here is my son, my only child. It was just blood all over. My anguish was beyond anything I ever thought I could experience. They have finished him. I threw myself down. I can feel the wetness of his blood — I felt his last breath leave him. He was my only child."

The event seemed so vivid to me that it was as if it were happening in the moment. Her use of tense defied the rules of grammar as she crossed and recrossed the boundaries of past and present in an illustration of the timelessness of traumatic pain, which Lawrence Langer has called "durational time": "He *ran* out. He *is* still chewing his bread. . . . *Now* I am dazed. I *ran*. . . ." And the final moment when she recalled seeing her son's lifeless body: "Here *is* my son." With a gesture of her hand she transformed the tragic scene from one that happened more than ten years earlier to one that we were witnessing right there on the floor of her front room.

Mrs. Plaatjie spoke of a world where helpless parents grieved because they couldn't protect their children inside or outside the home but could only cover up the memory of their grief and hope that someday grass would grow over it. For one brief moment on a sunny afternoon, she had brushed the grass back to let me see those deepest memories and the shards of pain that lay beneath. The pieces of that fateful day were still shattered, like broken china that cannot be put back together. The indelible images of her traumatized memory — the crumbs on top of the cupboard, the knife still smudged with uneaten peanut butter, the chair positioned exactly *there* — all these items had in her mind become symbols of her little Themba's final act at home, the last things he touched that were not covered in blood, that could be recovered as symbols of the objects that form the daily aesthetics of life. Even the image of the crumbs was treasured as a sacred memory.

Mrs. Plaatjie's memory of that day is recalled and represented by broken pieces, symbolizing the broken body of her son and her own broken dreams for his life. In a sense, the cupboard, the bread, the peanut butter, the knife are all crumbs, pieces that no longer fit together into a coherent whole or life story. But she nevertheless covets these crumbs and pieces because they are the only things in her memory of that day that are not spattered in blood. Words from T. S. Eliot's famous poem "The Waste Land" come to mind: "These fragments I have shored against my ruins." The image is of a broken person trying helplessly, not altogether with success, to recover some sense of coherence in an inner world that has become broken, a world where the ever-present trauma refuses to be silenced, to be buried under the grass.

As I sat through many public hearings of the TRC, in my role as panelist or as chair of the proceedings, I was struck by this idea of trauma as presence, trauma as *lived* memory.[9] So real were the images presented by witnesses that one was sucked in by the power of the relived experiences they recounted. The testimony of Yvonne Khutwane comes to mind. An anti-apartheid activist from Zwelethemba, the township in Worcester, she came to testify about her harassment by the police in 1986. She was arrested and thrown into the back of an army truck, where she found herself surrounded by young soldiers in camouflage uniform. She described her ordeal inside this lion's den: "One of the soldiers lifted my dress. As he reached for my panty, I became frightened, not knowing what he was going to do. He pushed his hand into my vagina. I had a mixture of emotions, but one that I remember clearly was a feeling of embarrassment, because his age — he was the same age as my children."

The image of a young white man violating such deeply personal boundaries evoked in a flash my own memory and fear in a near-rape experience more than twenty years before when I was a student at Fort Hare University. I was hitchhiking from Queenstown when a gray Mercedes-Benz with Port Elizabeth number plates driven by a pleasant-looking, well-dressed, middle-aged white man pulled up to give me a ride for what I thought would be the last leg of my trip to Cala, my hometown, since the man said he was going to Elliot. After a mildly interesting and innocuous conversation about university life — he had been at Rhodes University some years before — the man asked, "Do you want to go to Paradise with me?" "*Paradise?*" I asked, genuinely unaware of the sinister meaning behind the word, until he reached out and laid his hand on my hip, making my whole body turn with revulsion. (I was wearing the only pair of jeans I owned, and since then I have never worn jeans again.) His smile, which had seemed so friendly, turned into a monstrous sneer as he steered his car in the direction of a small forest concealing part of a lake just outside Queenstown. The car slowed down to negotiate the change of road surface, and on the spur of the moment I opened the passenger door and jumped out, rolling onto the gravel road. Shocked and terrified, I ran as fast as I could, not looking back.

As I listened to Mrs. Khutwane telling her story before a public audience of the TRC and to me as facilitator of her testimony, my heart started to beat violently. I imagined the detour in my nightmare ride and I reexperienced my own trauma in that near-tragedy. Then I pictured her in the back of the army truck, her body being violated by a white soldier in camouflage uniform, and I feel every detail of her trauma as if it is something that has happened to me: the intrusive hand of the young soldier, the shame of helplessness, and the humiliation all seem like a painful stab deep inside.

The feeling was so intense that I choked with tears. A fellow committee member next to me on the stage reached out to stroke my back to comfort me. The gesture brought me back to my senses, so to speak. I had to regain my composure. How could I fulfill my role on the TRC if I allowed myself to be affected by victims' testimonies? Forcing myself to return to the role of facilitator, I repeated something that Mrs. Khutwane had said earlier in her testimony, more like talking to myself in order to understand the full implication of the soldier's terribly wounding act than as a way to help Mrs. Khutwane tell her story: "The soldier could have been your child."

There were many other stories recounted on the TRC public stage that were real in a very personal way. Mr. Mzikhaya Mkabile, who is from Cala, the same small town where I grew up, was imprisoned on Robben Island, the Alcatraz of South Africa, where Nelson Mandela served most of his life sentence. Before his imprisonment, Mr. Mkabile lost his hearing through, and bears the scars of, the torture he suffered at the hands of the head of BOSS (Bureau of State Security), Hendrik Van den Bergh, and the two infamous warders of Robben Island, the Kleynhans brothers. Mr. Mkabile communicated only by lip-reading, and as facilitator of his testimony I sat next to him. He described his torture by the Kleynhans brothers. Mr. Mkabile and other prisoners were working in the Robben Island lime quarry, where Nelson Mandela injured his eyes. The brothers spotted him helping one of his comrades who had blisters on his hands. They made him dig a shallow grave and forced him to lie in it. Then they covered his body with sand up to the neck. Then Peter Kleynhans opened his fly and urinated into Mr. Mkabile's nose. As if sensing that the audience didn't believe him, sensing what Lawrence Langer has called "the vast imaginative space" separating what he had endured from the audience's capacity to absorb it,[10] Mr. Mkabile said, "Let me show you." Now he was standing, facing the audience and the commissioners. He made a gesture demonstrating someone opening his fly and pointing an imaginary penis in the air. He described again how Peter Kleynhans had urinated in his nose. "Because I couldn't breathe, I opened my mouth" — he opened his mouth, still standing — "and swallowed his urine while breathing through the mouth."[11]

Mkabile then sat down and, in response to a question I asked, pointed out one by one each of the physical scars of his torture, identifying each scar with the name of the torturer: Van den Bergh! Peter Kleynhans! The impotent rage written on his face as he called out the names of his former torturers brought back childhood memories of my father's impotent anger whenever we were stopped and searched by a young white policeman on one of our annual family trips from Cape Town to my father's parents' home in the Eastern Cape. These memories, and other personal experiences of humiliation simply because of my skin color, which I had hardly dealt with in my life, had to be suppressed to enable me to do the work I was assigned on the TRC. I had developed a strategy for doing this. As victims gave their testimonies in Xhosa, I tried to capture the heart of the moment by elaborating on my own English translation of their statements. I was documenting my witness to the historical moment when victims broke their silence at last. The writing distanced me from having to feel the pain of those who came to tell their stories to the commission, as if this would keep my own feelings at bay.

At the end of the Worcester hearings, Mrs. Khutwane had looked for me to tell me how healing she had found my show of emotion during her testimony. "I felt you were connecting with my pain at a deep level, and that someone understood what I went through," she explained.

Being on the commission reopened for me the multiple meanings of a childhood, a student's life, and a professional life under apartheid South Africa. I was not a neutral listener on the commission, a "blank screen."[12] This was true for many of us on the commission. It was something we had to be aware of in order to exercise reasonable judgment in the process of making our findings about the cases that were presented to the Human Rights Violations Committee.[13] The commission emphasized evenhandedness. Any demonstration of emotion was interpreted as proof of bias.[14] Dealing with victims' traumatic memories that evoked one's own memory of the past without letting go of one's emotions was no easy feat. As a result, many of us who served on the TRC — those who took statements from victims, the briefers, the commissioners, the investigators, and the interpreters — continue to struggle with closure, in part because we had to deny our own emotions in order to contain the pain of the victims who appeared before us.[15]

I have mentioned another extraordinary encounter with victims of atrocity. I am thinking of the meeting between de Kock and the widows of the two policemen murdered in the Motherwell bombing. Pearl Faku responded to de Kock's apology with the fullness of her humanity, saying: "I hope that when he sees our tears, he knows that they are not only tears for our husbands, but tears for him as well. . . . I would like to hold him by the hand, and show him that there is a future, and that he can still change." Her statement of forgiveness was profound. As an invitation to de Kock to turn the page, to come onto the path toward the road of peace, it had no equal that I was aware of on the TRC, nor was I aware of any such gestures made by victims in the history of atrocities in the twentieth century. Her response surpasses much of what we know about people who have been victimized when their victimizers ask forgiveness. It is hard to resist the conclusion that there must be something divine about forgiveness expressed in the context of tragedy. How else can we understand how such words can flow from the lips of one wronged so irreparably? Archbishop Tutu, whenever we were witnesses to such inexplicable human responses at a public hearing of the TRC, would be driven to call for silence "because we are on holy ground." There seems to be something spiritual, even sacramental, about forgiveness — a sign that moves and touches those who are witnesses to its enactment.

We might ask, what does Pearl Faku forgive de Kock for? For bringing about the death of her husband? For crossing the threshold of morality and allowing his evil to prevail and to contemplate, plan, and commit such a deed? In offering de Kock her forgiveness, did she mean to say, "I forgive you for being so malicious, so perverted, so indescribably wicked as to have committed this abhorrent act that has robbed my children of a father and robbed me of a husband"?

I doubt that when forgiveness is offered, the gaze is cast on the specifics of the deed. Forgiveness, while not disregarding the act, begins not with it but with the person. Forgiveness recognizes the deed, its impact having been and continuing to be lived by the victim, but transcends it. People who come to the point of forgiveness have lived not only with the pain that trauma and loss bring, but also with the anger and resentment at those who caused the pain. That is their reality — a world of painful emotional wounds, hostility, and resentment at the injustice visited upon them. All these emotions connect them to their loved ones and so are a force that provides continuity and defies death, sustaining their bonds with those they loved who are now dead. The hateful emotions therefore recast the lost loved one as the living dead — "living," through the link maintained by the hateful affect. Paradoxically, these emotions also tie the individual to the one who inflicted the traumatic wounds. In fact, the hateful emotions may sometimes take on a life of their own, exerting considerable power over the victim.

The presence of resentful emotions does not necessarily mean that the person is willfully "holding on" to hatred. The victim is holding on to what seems to be the only connection to the one who is no longer present. This happens, in part, unconsciously. It is simply that the person who has suffered gross violations of human rights has lived with resentment too long to be able to let go of it easily. At the same time, such emotions are a burden that prevent the victim from fully coming to terms with the trauma and moving on. In this sense, these emotions may be seen as serving contradictory functions: as a connection with the loved one, they are symbolic of continuity; as a symbol of the perpetrator's powerful grip over the victim, they are a burden that hangs over the victim and at once creates a dependency on the hateful emotions and denies the victim a chance to come to terms with what happened.

Nyameka Goniwe, whose husband, Matthew Goniwe, was one of the anti-apartheid leaders brutally killed by the Eastern Cape security police, expressed disappointment at the lack of truth in a hearing investigating her husband's killers. "I can't forgive and forget, or go on with my life until I know the actual killers," she said. Speaking on behalf of the other widows, she continued: "We cannot close this chapter yet. Our lives have been involved in this case for years. I don't know how it feels to be without it."[16]

Do the emotions associated with the trauma become part of the identity of the one who has suffered loss? Traumatic experience ruptures a part of the victim's identity. It violates the boundaries that protect the definition of self, leaving the individual stripped of many of the things that bestow respect, dignity, and self-worth. Anger and resentment become the only personal "possessions" that the individual now has in place of the loved one. The emotions stand in the place of what was lost, and become an important part of the traumatized person's identity. Letting go of these emotions, if there is nothing new in the victim's life to strengthen her or him, makes the victim feel exposed and vulnerable again.

When forgiveness is granted, however, it is a choice the victim makes to let go of the bitterness. This usually occurs when there has been a change in the way the victim relates to his or her trauma. Forgiveness is not simply meant to relieve victimizers of their guilt, to make things easy for them. Such an interpretation makes forgiveness a further burden for victims. Forgiveness can also open up a new path toward healing for the victim. As Doreen Mgoduka said about granting de Kock forgiveness, "Now I can mourn properly because this has helped me retrace his [her husband's] steps in life in order to let him go in death." De Kock, for the policemen's widows, had "brought us the truth," which allowed them somehow to reconnect with their husbands.

Victims themselves sometimes seem to be looking for an opportunity to forgive, because they see this as something that can bring an end to a life of hatred, which ties them so inextricably to the perpetrator. One simply has to guard against prescribing forgiveness, for to do so cheapens the process. That first step taken, even to consider meeting a person responsible for terrible wrongs, is the victim's to take. When forgiveness is granted, it is probably because of the meaning the victim attaches to the perpetrator's apology. In a conversation I had with Nyameka Goniwe, I asked her to explain when, from a victim's perspective, is the moment to grant forgiveness to a perpetrator who seeks it. "Victims are looking for signs," she replied, "and when they see those signs, they are ready to forgive."[17]

While it is senseless to make generalizations about forgiveness, there are nevertheless important insights that can be gleaned from the examples that made the work of the Truth and Reconciliation Commission so extraordinary. One reason why it is difficult to generalize about forgiveness is that not all the witnesses who came to the commission were willing even to consider forgiveness as an option. By contrast, there were others who formulated statements of forgiveness the moment there was an opportunity to meet those who had brought them misery and pain, even before there was any indication of an apology on the part of the perpetrator.[18]

Forgiveness usually begins with the person who needs to be forgiven. This means that there must be something in the perpetrator's behavior, some "sign," that invites the victim's forgiveness. The most crucial sign is an expression of remorse. One begins to appreciate the magnitude of forgiveness when the "wrong" for which an apology is tendered is an atrocity. There is no comparison between atrocities and daily upsets that occur between partners, family members, and colleagues. But even atrocities call for an apology that is sincere, unencumbered by explanation or justification. A sincere apology does not divert attention from the self, such as those accompanied by a disclaimer: "I'm sorry that your sister was killed. Please understand that I was fighting to end the oppression of my people." Or "I apologize. But what I did happened because of the political climate of those days."

A genuine apology focuses on the feelings of the other rather than on how the one who is apologizing is going to benefit in the end. It seeks to acknowledge full responsibility for an act, and does not use self-serving language to justify the behavior of the person asking forgiveness. It must communicate, convey, and *perform* as a "speech act" that expresses a desire to right the relationship damaged through the actions of the apologizer.[19] A sincere apology does not seek to erase what was done. No amount of words can undo past wrongs. Nothing can ever reverse injustices committed against others. But an apology pronounced in the context of horrible acts has the potential for transformation. It clears or "settles" the air in order to begin reconstructing the broken connections between two human beings.[20]

To be able to "perform," an apology has to name the deed, acknowledge wrongdoing, and recognize the pain of the victim. Such an apology conveys a sense of regret and deeply felt remorse. "Saying it makes it so."[21] A remorseful apology inspires empathy and forgiveness. The words of Pearl Faku in response to de Kock's apology illustrate this deeply felt empathy for one who has done infinitely irreparable damage: "I hope that when he sees our tears, he knows that they are not only tears for our husbands, but tears for him as well."

Dori Laub illustrates the importance and power of that critical empathic connection between former enemies in his account of a survivor of the Holocaust who witnessed some of the worst atrocities during the war and lost many members of her family. At the end of the war, she participated in the hunting down and killing of Nazi collaborators. But when a German youth was captured and brought to her for her to take revenge on him, she ended up caring for him, cleaning and covering his wounds before handing him over as a POW. When asked why she had helped him she replied, "How could I kill him — he looked into my face and I looked into his."[22] Responding with empathy to one who has caused us pain falls

into the category of behavior that I have defined as the "paradox of remorse."[23] Empathy is a response to another person's
pain; even in the midst of tragedy, pain cannot be evil.

It may be that perpetrators, by receiving the forgiveness
they want, also regain some of the control they are used to,
particularly control over the victim. In other words, forgiveness may indirectly bestow power back on the perpetrator instead of empowering the victim and restoring some of the
power she or he lost during the moment of trauma. It is possible that the encounter favors the perpetrator, who, because
the victim is still struggling with asserting herself or himself
and her or his rights, has the advantage as a person used to being in control and so is able to define the agenda even while
asking forgiveness. The forgiveness then reawakens the victim's feelings of powerlessness instead of becoming a vehicle
for shifting the power dynamic. The erosion of a sense of individual rights and of the ability to make a claim on these rights
may run very deep in some victims. Powerlessness is the
affliction of the traumatized, to paraphrase Judith Herman.[24]
So some victims, not used to claiming their rights, may not be
able to express rage against the perpetrator even when the perpetrator no longer poses a real danger.

When gestures of forgiveness are enacted from a position
of weakness rather than one of strength, how should we assess
the encounter between victim and victimizer? It has been suggested that a victim's response of hatred and resentment is
a necessary prior condition for an expression of forgiveness,
and that people who show no resentment for the injustices
done to them lack self-respect.[25] But this is to judge victims,
who may have little or no control over their own sense of
disempowerment and helplessness, too harshly. They may be
acting out what they have internalized throughout the years

when they were denied rights and privileges. People who have been marginalized by an oppressive system may know nothing other than to shrink in the presence of those who embody power.[26] Saying that they lack self-respect in not being able to "stand up" to their former oppressors, who continue shamelessly to flaunt their power, fails to recognize the legacy of oppressive systems and just how much damage they leave behind in the lives of those who have suffered years of abuse.

A classic illustration of a gesture of forgiveness expressed from a position of weakness comes from the TRC public hearing that investigated the role of Winnie Madikizela-Mandela, the former wife of Nelson Mandela, and the Mandela Football Club in the torture and murder of young black activists in the Johannesburg township of Soweto — what came to be known as "the Winnie Hearing." The public focus on the activities of the Mandela Football Club began in January 1989, after the body of one of the youths, Stompie Seipei, was found in the outskirts of Soweto, infested with maggots. The investigation led the police to the activities of the Mandela Football Club. In a subsequent court hearing, evidence was given linking the killing of Seipei to events that had taken place in the home of Winnie Madikizela-Mandela.

Nine years after Stompie Seipei's body was discovered, Madikizela-Mandela, once the embodiment of suffering, resistance, survival, and all the images associated with the fight against apartheid, was questioned as a perpetrator on the stage of the TRC. Once a fearless spokesperson for truth, she had become the bearer of secrets from the past. Once loved as "the Mother of the Nation," Madikizela-Mandela was caricatured by cartoonists as an evil woman with blood on her hands. This was one of the saddest stories in the history of the anti-apartheid resistance. At the end of the public hearing, during which

Madikizela-Mandela essentially denied any knowledge of what had been happening in her own backyard, and offered no meaningful apology, she approached Stompie Seipei's mother while the TV cameras rolled. With a triumphant smile and open arms, she embraced her. I watched the moment of contact between the two women: the mother's humble smile and return of the gesture, and Madikizela-Mandela's triumphant smile, enacting her imposing power through her embrace. Two smiles: one a symbol of power, and the other a symbol of impotence.

Stompie Seipei's bereaved mother had sat for nine days at the public hearing of the TRC looking silence in the face as Madikizela-Mandela revealed nothing, ending where she had started, with more silence. Yet she opened her arms to receive the embrace of this woman who was prepared to offer nothing beyond flat denial. It was an embrace that stripped the victim of what we call dignity, the reverse of what the TRC public hearings were meant to do.

The mistake is to see the political as separate from the personal — to see discontinuities between them. In dealing with the past, the narratives that people construct about what happened to them, the stories of their suffering, reflect the continuities between their personal and their political lives. The stories are about what they have experienced and continue to experience in a society in which the promised changes are not yet a reality for them. Therefore, some of the victims who encounter perpetrators cannot make that psychological leap and recognize that the tables have turned, that now the power is theirs to demand what is rightfully due them.

For those who have been privileged all their lives and have no problem demanding their rights, forgiveness may be seen as giving up their rights. By showing forgiveness, they may feel that they are relinquishing that infallibility, that superior stance that allows them to continue to punish the wrongdoer with their anger. Often this is accompanied by feelings of self-righteousness, which unfortunately cannot be relied on to promote reconciliation and transformation. Ironically, some of the feelings associated with powerlessness, such as humility, are more likely to foster an attitude of forgiveness than are attitudes that equate forgiveness with a loss of power.

South Africans face the challenge of how to embrace the past without being swallowed by the tide of vengeful thinking. The Truth and Reconciliation Commission was a strategy not only for breaking the cycle of politically motivated violence but also for teaching important lessons about how the human spirit can prevail even as victims remember the cruelty visited upon them in the past. If memory is kept alive in order to cultivate old hatreds and resentments, it is likely to culminate in vengeance, and in a repetition of violence. But if memory is kept alive in order to transcend hateful emotions, then remembering can be healing.

There are many people who find it hard to embrace the idea of forgiveness. And it is easy to see why. In order to maintain some sort of moral compass, to hold on to some sort of clear distinction between what is depraved but conceivable and what is simply off the scale of human acceptability, we feel an inward emotional and mental pressure *not* to forgive, since forgiveness can signal acceptability, and acceptability signals some amount, however small, of condoning. There is a desire to draw a line and say, "Where you have been, I cannot follow you. Your actions can never be regarded as part of what it means to be human." Yet not to forgive means closing the door to the possibility of transformation.

6 ⬇

Apartheid of the Mind

ASHORT DISTANCE away from a long dirt road that winds through sprawling acres of farmland, dry veld, and hills partially hidden by winter smog lies what was once the apartheid government's headquarters for death squads. As I caught my first glimpse of the farmhouse, the three brick barracks built some distance from it, and the expanse of wide-open land that surrounds it, I was struck by the picture of tranquillity, and by the realization that this place, Vlakplaas, just outside Pretoria, was the ideal setting for the concealment of some of the more gruesome schemes that the apartheid government constructed as part of its plan to destroy the bodies and minds of its enemies.

I drove to Vlakplaas following a map Eugene de Kock had drawn for me during an earlier meeting at the prison. Apprehensive about visiting the death farm, even under the benign management of its new post-apartheid caretakers, I asked my sister, Sesi, who was in Johannesburg on business, to accompany me. Sesi sat in the passenger seat and tried to read de Kock's map. "If you ask me, this is more about de Kock's own ambivalence than it is a map to Vlakplaas," she said cynically. "He wants you to see the place, to give you some perspective on these . . . *operations*. At the same time, he doesn't want you to see his House of Murder, and these directions are proof," she said, flicking her fingers repeatedly against the sheet of paper.

"The idea of your actually going to see Vlakplaas is new in your conversation with him, right? I mean, Vlakplaas as a concrete place that actually exists, right? It's unexplored; and he's frightened. Look at the tremor in his letters."

My sister was no handwriting analyst, but we were indeed getting lost using de Kock's directions. We couldn't even find the exit to Vlakplaas. Driving in circles, we finally decided to stop at a restaurant that had a church and recreation center attached to it. I approached a young woman behind the cash register, mid-twenties I would say, who was talking with a second, older woman, and asked if she could please direct us to Vlakplaas. "You mean *the* Vlakplaas?" she asked with a short, nervous laugh. She pointed to her companion, who, it turned out, lived close to Vlakplaas. The older woman, perhaps in her late fifties, was elegantly dressed, heavily jeweled, and spoke with a German accent. Vlakplaas, she explained, was a large farm divided into three separate plots. She and her sister often walked through one section of Vlakplaas, *ja*. But they knew nothing about what had gone on during those early years — about what had now come out in the papers.[1] All they knew was that part of Vlakplaas was a police barracks. That's all. How awful it all was. Vlakplaas is a beautiful farm with a glorious stream running through it. In fact, she and her sister wanted to buy this whole section of Vlakplaas, but unfortunately it was still government property.

What, I wondered, would their plans be for a farm with such a tarnished history if they were able to buy it?

Oh, she said, they wanted to convert it into a game reserve. Private, of course. It would be a wonderful symbol, don't you think, to have the vibrancy of living things in a place associated with death. *Ja,* there were bodies secretly buried there, that much she was aware of. But the souls of the people killed there would finally have a chance to rest in peace if the beauty of Vlakplaas were somehow restored. And what better way to do this than to have a game reserve right there? She could see deer frolicking against the backdrop of the beautiful hills. Out of the ashes of the dead can spring new life! Her eyes glinted and her jewelry clicked softly as she made hand gestures to convey her point.

As we drove through the final suburb before Vlakplaas, we passed an Indian couple standing in their garden in front of their house. I was curious to find out what their response would be to a request for directions to Vlakplaas, so I stopped and asked them. "Never heard of it," the man said. "Never heard of it." I looked at the woman. She too shook her head as our eyes met. We were literally seven minutes from Vlakplaas and they claimed not to know where it was or even what it was — neither the legitimate Vlakplaas farm nor the death camp that bore its name. Curiosity satisfied, I shifted into gear and pulled away.

Vlakplaas, the section we were interested in, was sealed off behind a tall fence with a large gate, clearly built to keep out unwanted guests. A pack of bulldogs charged aggressively as I got out of the car, barking and jumping up against the locked gate. A white woman stood in the distance, watching the commotion. She sent a young black man, apparently an employee, to talk to us. After speaking to him, I called out to the woman, who seemed unprepared to have a conversation with me. "All I can tell you," she shouted from several yards away, barely audible because of her barking dogs, "is that you have to make an appointment through the Department of Public Works to come in here."

Well, did she have the name of someone I could call right now on my cell phone and make these arrangements? No, she said. Her husband was the only person here who communicated with the department.

There was nothing to do but leave. Vlakplaas may no longer be the playground of politicians and generals taking pleasure in hatching new ways to dismember the human body and soul, but there was still something haunting about the farmhouse and the three ugly little buildings next to it. Vlakplaas was as inscrutable, as impregnable, as it had ever been in de Kock's time.

"What was your life like outside of Vlakplaas?" I asked de Kock. "Were your children, your wife aware of what you were doing when you left them every morning for work?"

"It was hell. But they never knew. It was hell all the way. I mean, I was permanently armed with one firearm on my ankle and another on the hip. Even when I went to a shopping mall with them. Sometimes I had my sports bag over my shoulder: the Uzi was in there. It's not that you can use three firearms at a time. But being disabled in using one, you would use the next, you know, things like that. It wasn't a matter of paranoia. It was the reality of this life. Especially when everything was now coming out in the open."

He spoke matter-of-factly, but I could sense from his unfocused gaze that his mind was back there, back in the heat of apartheid's urban warfare. "I was afraid of my own people, *my own people*, because now they knew where I was, where I worked, when I left home, and where I would be at a specific time. If I slipped up in the least, we were gone, my whole family. I go on holiday with an Uzi in the one bag. The truth is that Vlakplaas had been exposed and we didn't trust one another. What has happened to your enemy can happen to you if you become the enemy."

He looked old, or perhaps just tired from the stress of the last several years, but the fire of survival still burned in his eyes, as if he had become used to staying just one step ahead of death, one body length away from a land mine or a sniper's bullet.

"You were just grateful that something didn't happen in the past," he continued, "and the future was a sort of a tornado, you know, well, a vortex. You couldn't see into that, and now could be the time. Are the children all right now? Is there someone lurking over there? Is that the ice cream van or is it not? It was small things you were worried about. You were too scared. If you were in a restaurant with the children, you went with them to the toilet and you brought them back. You just couldn't take a chance. You didn't. I was eventually more afraid of my own people than I was of the ANC or the PAC, because I knew them and I knew what they could do. I knew what I had done. It could happen to me."

De Kock's experience of his own life at this time as concealed from his wife and family and as separate from "my own people" — who might kill him at any time — is reflective of the whole idea of apartheid, the compartmentalization of South African thinking. There were two South Africas: white and black. Similarly, there was the public world and the private world, the open and the covert. And they were rigidly separate. What happened under cover of covert action was fine, so long as it did not come out in the open. The two spheres were not to collide. White South African bystanders were able to live with the brutality against blacks because it was being carried out in relative secret, in that "other" world. Everyone engaged in an "apartheid of the mind," in psychological splitting. It was only when the truth came out in the open that some felt they could no longer live with it. Then, the veil of silence was maintained for the greater good.

"You were doing something important. But it's not a life," de Kock continued. "It's not even an existence. You are in some twilight world of no peace, no rest, no trust, nothing. *Nothing, nothing, nothing, nothing.*" I wondered if he were taking stock of a life that he felt could ultimately be summed up in that one word. "At the end of the day you are basically your only friend, and then your wife, and your kids."

"What did your children think you were doing? Leaving home every morning — you must have told them something. And what about the Uzi in your bag, all these guns in their lives? Did they ever ask?"

"Never. I mean, not in a way that children do, trying to get information. They never knew that I was a policeman because I never wore a uniform, and even the oldest one, from when he was quite small he would say, 'Daddy is a businessman.' And then the youngest one even: 'He's a businessman.' They saw other people in uniform; they'd say, 'That's a policeman.' But to them I'm a businessman. They never knew."

De Kock's wife and two sons left South Africa to resettle in a country de Kock won't disclose. In his story narrated to Jeremy Gordin, de Kock says that his wife asked him for a divorce. Although I have never questioned him directly about it, it may well be true. Or the claim may be de Kock's way of protecting himself and his family against future retaliatory actions by disassociating his family from his own guilt through creating an alleged emotional barrier. I couldn't say for sure, but it was clear from his conversations about his family that their safety was foremost in his mind and that he would do all he could to protect them. That is not, however, to discount reports of some families breaking up as a result of the outpouring of graphic evidence from the Truth Commission hearings.[2]

I wondered whether these breakups occurred because the wives recoiled from the morally reprehensible nature of their husbands' actions, or because they felt they couldn't endure the public shame their husbands had brought upon the family. In many cases I suspect the latter was the controlling factor — that the publicity was the greater discomfort. Although many of the men — like people all over the world involved in their governments' secret operations — went to great lengths to compartmentalize their existence and to separate their covert work from their family life, it is more likely than not that many wives knew or suspected that as members of the security police, their husbands were involved in the mysterious murders, tortures, and disappearances of anti-apartheid activists but were content to remain officially in the dark about the real nature of their husbands' work.

Tacitly or openly, most white people supported the regime of terror as something grim but good. After all, the police were only killing "communists" to protect the state. It would be hard to believe that it was only when these crimes came to public light that white people suddenly realized that what had happened under apartheid was terrible. De Kock and many of the apartheid government's operatives have said repeatedly that what kept them going — what sustained their zeal and conviction in the rightness of crushing the heads of thousands of black activists — was the tacit but powerful support they felt they were receiving from the beneficiaries of apartheid

privilege — the polite churchgoers, the cultured suburban-
ites, the voters. It is at their feet that the responsibility for
apartheid, ultimately, can be laid.

"White society had a good life," de Kock said, sneering, as if
there was something repulsive about the idea. "They were
quite happy with what they got, and now they are not so
happy with who made it happen. I mean, how many whites really voted against the National Party? Whites say they didn't
know, but did they want to know? As long as they were now
safe and they had their nice houses and their second cars and
their third cars and their swimming pools and kids at good
government schools and university, they had no problem with
cross-border raids and other counterinsurgency operations of
the security. Cross-border raids were so well publicized; why
did they never question this?"

De Kock was clearly angry that he had been made a scape-
goat — that while he had been sought after as a master counterinsurgency strategist and treated like a hero under apartheid, he had become the most despised white person in post-
apartheid South Africa.

There are others like de Kock who believed at the time in the
moral rightness of apartheid but who are now faced with the
question of what it was they were fighting for, and what it
was they were expected to die for. One of the most compelling
statements submitted to the TRC, by a former conscript
whose brother was killed in Namibia, raised just such a question. Owen McGregor wanted to know from the former apartheid leaders: Why did my brother die?

My TRC colleagues and I came across the report on the
death of Wallace McGregor in a community newspaper, the
Paarl Post, when we were making preparations for public
hearings in the Western Cape winelands region town of Paarl.

It was a short paragraph about a young man "killed in action" in Namibia in March 1987. With the help of one of the newspaper's reporters, Suzanne Botha, I telephoned Wallace McGregor's mother and asked if she would like to share with the TRC her son's experiences and the events that led to his death.[3]

When I met Mrs. Anne Marie McGregor in her social worker's office in Paarl, I found the same pained eyes that I had witnessed among many black women who had lost their children violently. Mrs. McGregor had been unable to see her son's body, which was brought home in a body bag, following the tradition of the military code. Nor was anyone allowed to disclose the circumstances of Wallace's death. Mrs. McGregor had suffered ten agonizing years of uncertainty, "seeing" Wallace in every young man in the street who bore any resemblance to him, hoping that one day Wallace would appear at her door — knowing, yet not knowing, that the body in the bag had been her son's. Mrs. McGregor's two surviving sons, Owen and Robert, had also apparently not been able to deal with the cloud of secrecy surrounding their brother's death.

Shortly before the public proceedings in Paarl began, a TRC staff member handed me Owen McGregor's statement. What was remarkable about Owen's written submission was that in it he had made his dead brother, Wallace, the narrator of the testimony, and himself its subject. At the top of the page Owen stated that what followed was what he thought his brother would have said had he, Owen, been the one killed in the army. As I read out the testimony, I was overwhelmed by this symbolic act of reversal.

"My name is Matthew William Wallace McGregor," the dead man spoke from the grave through his brother's written statement:

My brother is dead today and I can think of no good reason why. What did he know about politics? All he knew
were the lies. He was told that there were forty thousand
Cuban soldiers wanting to invade South Africa, that the
blacks of Namibia were communists and wanted to take
over South Africa, and that there was a small rebel group
called the ANC. My brother did not have time to learn
that these were all lies. According to him, he died a hero
because that's all he knew. I regret that he did not live
long enough — my brother — to know the truth. I want
you to know my brother that the people you defended
against the ANC all along supported the ANC. The ANC
was never a little rebel group. It was the people of South
Africa. I want to ask the National Party if they thought
they could get away with these lies. I want them to know
that now we all know the truth. To P. W. Botha and his
cabinet of those days, why did my brother die? Explain
to my mother and my father and to all South Africans
how and why my brother died. Why did I die? Regards,
Wallace.

Giving a dead person a voice, entering the silence of the
grave, is a profound act of symbolism. It is a kind of sacrificial
act: trading places with the other and "dying" in his place.
Owen McGregor's testimony is as much about responsibility
for a brother's memory as it is about confronting the leaders of
the former apartheid government. *"Why did I die?"* It's a metaphor for the silence of many white South Africans, as if their
voices can be heard only through the speech of the dead.

De Kock had committed his crimes in the name of white society. White people could escape the ravages of the past and
leave it "behind" or "buried." But de Kock's past was following him. *He* was paying his price in shame. In all my meetings

with de Kock, I hadn't seen this more cogently than in one of my later visits with him at Pretoria Prison. It was April 1998. As usual my conversation with de Kock had gone beyond the time I was allowed to stay at the prison, and two guards came to the door to tell me my time was up. Usually de Kock was the first to apologize and to get up to leave with one guard as another waited for me to collect my belongings. But today, as I put my tape recorder, pens, and notebook in my bag, I noticed that de Kock was still lingering, as if he had something to say but did not quite know how to say it. Although I continued to get ready to leave, I was stalling to see how he would handle his uncertainty. De Kock came over and stood in front of me, arms folded and shoulders raised in a stiff, tense posture. He first looked away, then looked back at me, biting his lower lip as if about to admit to something terrible he had done. A heavy silence hung in the room. "Pumla," he began. "I've been meaning to ask you this, right from our second interview. Have I ever killed any of your friends or family?"

The words bounced around the large room like an echo in a cave. I actually turned and looked around, expecting perhaps to see someone else in the room other than the guards at the door. Yes, I had heard de Kock's voice. I was sure that was what I'd heard . . . but had I just imagined it? Standing there stunned, in conversation with a broken man who had been an angel of death, I felt as if I were in the midst of a collision of scattered meanings within these prison walls that had enclosed our conversations. De Kock's words hovered in the room: I was struggling to understand them before I could take them in.

I looked at de Kock, searching deep within his eyes, reading between the lines for signs of evil, of malice. His eyes were filled with suffering. I felt nothing but pity, the kind one feels when a friend is in pain over an event that has deeply troubled him. I stared at his face again, and for a moment I thought I might touch him — *again?* — to offer him some respite from the tortured emotions that seemed to be coursing through his brain and body. But how? Where could I touch him? The awkwardness of reaching out to someone, almost six feet tall, who had killed many of my people, and to do it in front of the black guards, who I doubted had heard de Kock's question in the large, echoing room but were still standing at the door holding it open and watching. What would *they* think? What would de Kock think? This black woman reaching out to him with an embrace? De Kock stood in front of me, his shoulders bearing the weight of struggling with the memory of his own evil. I felt then that even if de Kock had killed my loved ones, I would never have been able to tell him. I would have had to spare him. There was something in his face that I hadn't seen before, something utterly despairing. I finally found my voice. I said to him, "No, Eugene. No one close to me."

It is possible that de Kock was able to find some solace in those words, some small window of opportunity to salvage a sense of having done something right for once in a life gone to waste. But *I* cannot absolve de Kock from what he did. That role belongs to those whose lives he cut short — his victims — and to those they left behind. "Have I ever killed any of your loved ones?" Ultimately, what I heard was the voice of an outcast begging to rejoin the world of the living. His past, it seems, was unbearable. But his future, stained as it was with the memory of lives snuffed out, was also unbearable.

As de Kock's words reverberated in my head on the drive back to Johannesburg, I thought of one of the unforgettable voices I had heard during the Truth Commission hearings, a survivor of torture at the hands of Jeffrey Benzien, a former apartheid security policeman. "What kind of a person are you?" asked Tony Yengeni, a former ANC cadre, as he faced his torturer on the TRC stage. What kind of a man was de Kock? What kind was he then? What kind is he now?

On the day of my last interview with de Kock, in April 1998, he described in detail how the apartheid government's intelligence network operated through the different covert units; how victims were disabled or killed by secret poisoning — drinks laced with fatal drugs — or explosives sent with correspondence or with "gifts" — clothing, letters, Walkman radios, pens. Later that morning, as I was standing in a queue at the Home Affairs Department to collect my new passport, a young white man at the end of the line approached me and asked to borrow my pen. This seemed odd to me, that a man would jump ahead of so many people to ask me for a pen. There was nothing overtly suspicious about him; he looked ordinary. But it was this ordinary demeanor that aroused a sense of anxiety. Had this man followed me from the prison? Did he want to harm me, to exchange my pen for one fitted with explosives? But why should he hurt me? Suddenly I was filled with an uncontrollable sense of fear, and of anger at being gripped by what I *knew* was an irrational emotion. I watched this man carefully, but not openly, as he went to the counter to fill out a form. These people can be very swift, I thought to myself. I may not notice when he swaps the pens.

I knew I was imagining things. But as I walked out of the Home Affairs building, my pen having been returned to me, I threw it into a trash can on the street.

When I arrived in the United States that summer, I braced myself for the tapes and transcripts of the interviews with de Kock. Alone with this material, thousands of miles from the streets of Pretoria, I was afraid, not of the memory of the evil schemes that were concocted in that city but of my own empathy for de Kock.[4]

7 ⬇

"I Have No Hatred in My Heart"

Aᴌᴛʜᴏᴜɢʜ ꜰᴏʀɢɪᴠᴇɴᴇss is often regarded as an expression of weakness, the decision to forgive can paradoxically elevate a victim to a position of strength as the one who holds the key to the perpetrator's wish. For just at the moment when the perpetrator begins to show remorse, to seek some way to ask forgiveness, the victim becomes the gatekeeper to what the outcast desires — readmission into the human community. And the victim retains that privileged status as long as he or she stays the moral course, refusing to sink to the level of the evil that was done to her or to him. In this sense, then, forgiveness is a kind of revenge, but revenge enacted at a rarefied level. Forgiving may appear to condone the offense, thus further disempowering the victim. But forgiveness does not overlook the deed: it rises above it. "This is what it means to be human," it says. "I cannot and will not return the evil you inflicted on me." And that is the victim's triumph.

I sometimes sensed this feeling of triumph myself while visiting de Kock. I felt a sense of power over him as a person who needed my understanding — that in his remorse, and behind all of his psychological defenses, he was a human being pleading to be understood, desperate, in fact, for someone to help him understand *himself*. I felt, indeed, a distinct moral satisfaction that I was not like the de Kock of the apartheid days, and that allowing myself to feel anger or bitterness toward him would chip away at and ultimately destroy that distinction. There was nothing as satisfying as returning from an interview with de Kock and realizing that I could not regard him with the same dehumanizing hatred and disdain that he had trained on his victims. In fact, I did not want hatred to make *me* his victim. I knew in a profound way that somehow that was the right thing to do — both for myself and for him.

Stories of forgiveness from victims of human rights abuses, like that of Amy Biehl's parents, Peter and Linda Biehl,[1] are significant not only because they mark some of the most memorable moments and moral achievements in the life of the TRC hearings, but also, even more important, because they translate the forgiveness model from high-minded homily to actual practice, from what is conceivable in principle to what has worked. They lay a path, an already trodden path, making it possible to know that it is within the grasp of ordinary people to forgive evil and to end generational cycles of violence.

The question is no longer *whether* victims can forgive "evildoers" but whether we — our symbols, language, and politics, our legal, media, and academic institutions — are creating the conditions that encourage alternatives to revenge. We have come to rely too narrowly on retribution as the only legitimate form of justice and on the Nuremberg trial model as the only one capable of adequately addressing state-orchestrated atrocities. Tellingly, recent international tribunals such as the International Criminal Tribunal on the genocide in Rwanda and the tribunal in The Hague on the former

Yugoslavia have run into problems. In Rwanda, for example, victims have felt largely excluded from a process that is supposed to help heal their wounds and restore some normality in their society.[2] Our knowledge of the dynamic between victims and perpetrators has further been influenced by narratives from the Holocaust experience. Although a few Jewish German groups have been established to try to build positive relationships between children of Holocaust survivors and descendants of Nazi perpetrators,[3] Holocaust discourse has sometimes emphasized remembering but not so clearly dialogue,[4] which is critical if victims are to live again with perpetrators in the same society, or indeed if they are to live in greater harmony with themselves.

Dialogue, of course, will not solve every problem faced by a society that has suffered sustained violence on a large scale. But dialogue does create avenues for broadening our models of justice and for healing deep fractures in a nation by unearthing, acknowledging, and recording what has been done. It humanizes the dehumanized and confronts perpetrators with their inhumanity. Through dialogue, victims as well as the greater society come to recognize perpetrators as human beings who failed morally, whether through coercion, the perverted convictions of a warped mind, or fear.

Far from relieving the pressure on them, recognizing the most serious criminals as human intensifies it, because society is thereby able to hold them to greater moral accountability. Indeed, demonizing as monsters those who commit evil lets them off too easily. Managed carefully, dialogue condemns — but not too hastily, lest it foreshorten the accountability process and, perversely, excuse the criminal by dismissing him into the category of the hopelessly, radically other. Sustained, engaged, ordered dialogue thus forces an offender to unearth what moral sensibilities he has buried under a facade of "obedience to orders" or righteous "duty to my country" and to face what he has done, not in the heady climate of the period of mayhem but in the sobering atmosphere of reflection on ordinary human lives now shattered. But it also thereby invites him, if he can, if he dare, to negotiate the chasm between his monstrousness and the world of the forgiven. It thus encourages him to stop denying the suspected truth: that all along, he knew that he was human and knew right from wrong.[5] The act of humanizing is therefore at once both punishment and rehabilitation. Finally, dialogue creates the possibility of setting the person's actions, through testimony and witnessing, in the broader framework of the political-ideological context that may have supported and even directed his deeds. It is this component of the crime, the one that resides at the systemic, institutional, and policy levels rather than at a personal level, that is notoriously difficult to substantiate within the strict evidentiary rules of a purely judicial process. Thus the politics of abuse that were enshrined in the policies of an oppressive system can be acknowledged and confirmed in ways that the more rigid, adversarial relationship of courtroom exchanges cannot.

Feelings of anger and revenge against those who commit gross abuses are, understandably, easier to develop and to sustain than an attitude that seeks engagement and dialogue. One reason we distance ourselves through anger from those who have hurt us or others we know is the fear that if we engage them as real people, we will be compromising our moral stance and lowering the entry requirements into the human community. Part of my own struggle in my visits with de Kock stemmed from my fear of stepping into the shoes of a murderer through empathy.

This discomfort was at times overwhelmingly intense, especially during the incident when I spontaneously reached out to touch de Kock. It was present with equal intensity when I started using his first name, and he mine. I could not quite articulate why. In the black township where I grew up, younger people never called adults by their first name. In fact, children felt uneasy referring to an adult by first name even among others their age, or even when a friendly adult, a young teacher, for instance, invited them to do it. Yet I am sure that my discomfort in addressing de Kock by his first name — my discomfort in simply *saying* his name in his presence — had little to do with my childhood conditioning.

De Kock's last name had passed into public usage almost as a household term, shorthand for apartheid's henchman par excellence. In using his last name, I could take refuge behind the voices of the entire community. Besides, it was his family name, one he shared with relatives, many of whom I presumed were decent people. It was not simply *his* name. But his first name — that was the *real* him. And *that* — despite all of my reflection and theorizing about forgiveness, despite my desire to reach beyond instinctual feelings of revulsion against the executors of apartheid's Total Onslaught and to see him in a fresh light, a higher light, as an evil person, yes, but a person nonetheless — was what I had real difficulty coming to terms with.

"*Of course* it should make you uncomfortable!" said Heribert Adam, the Canadian sociologist, when I told him about this.[6] "Can you imagine anyone referring to Hitler as 'Adolf'?" What Adam missed, and what I had experienced firsthand, is the enormous distinction between Hitler — or those tried at Nuremberg, for that matter — and de Kock and others who appeared before the TRC: none of the Nazis gave any evidence of even a trace of remorse.[7] Genuine remorse and regret over destroying lives and severing the relationships that were connected to them make all the difference. These are emotions that, despite the evil committed, are not themselves evil. What remains significant is that in spite of de Kock's remorse, even though he was standing at the door and knocking, I still felt uncomfortable with the idea of letting him in, of reinstating the human bond between him and me.

There always seem to be unasked questions about my work with de Kock written on people's faces whenever I discuss my interview visits. What draws me to this evil man? they want to know. Am I like the scores of admirers who wrote to Richard Ramirez, the "Night Stalker," on San Quentin's death row, including magazine editor Doreen Lioy, who began by corresponding with him and ended up marrying him?[8] Do I find evil attractive and mysteriously intoxicating, like Esmarelda (Angela Jones), the female taxicab passenger in Quentin Tarantino's *Pulp Fiction*, who asks the fleeing boxer Butch (Bruce Willis) provocatively: "What does it feel like? Killing a man. . . . I want to know what it feels like to *kill* a man"?[9] Or is it a desire to tame and nurture a problem man, or to take on the project of rehabilitating a dangerous and incorrigible killer in order to work out my own proclivities toward evil on the external canvas of an other?

For many people those questions remained tactfully unasked. But Heribert was not going to hold back. "Are you in love with him?" he inquired.

It was interesting to see how some people struggled, not with the content of my conversations with de Kock, but with the fact that I could be talking to him at all in the first place. Romantic interest seemed to carry greater explanatory power for conversing with a murderous criminal than compassion. Others used the word "fascination," as in, "Are you fascinated with him?" Perhaps the most cautious of these comments came from a UCLA psychology professor friend of mine, Steve Lopez. Steve listened intently as I described some highlights of my work with de Kock, then looked at me searchingly and said, "He must be a very good-looking man."

Casting my professional interest in de Kock in terms of a romantic motive ("in love with him") or as something mysterious ("She's so fascinated by him!") makes it too easy for my listeners to distance themselves from the reality of interacting with the man. It allows them to dismiss my work as something unnatural, something kinky. It allows them to set it aside — to set *me* aside — as an exception, something allowable within the space of soap opera irrationality, something on someone else's screen. There is a charming madness to it. It closes off the possibility of any serious dialogue on the real subject of my visits to the C section of Pretoria Central Prison: to understand the inner mind of evil, to follow its thought processes, and to expose myself to its human face, stripped of media stereotypes and the easy distance of hatred. Connecting on a human level with a monster therefore comes to be a profoundly frightening prospect, for ultimately, it forces us to confront the potential for evil within ourselves. Compassion toward and hence forgiveness of people who have left a gruesome trail in their wake in effect brings "innocent" victims and wicked men together to share at a single common table of humanity, and that prospect is unpalatable.[10]

Hannah Arendt writes that "radically evil" acts "transcend the realm of human affairs" and are therefore neither punishable nor forgivable."[11] The radically evil are unpunishable because no amount of punishment can balance what they have done. They are unforgivable because no yardstick exists by which we can measure what it means to forgive them, and there is no mental disposition we can adopt toward them that would correct the sense of injustice that their actions have injected into our world.

On the scale of horrible things that can happen to people,

there are some for which the language of apology and forgiveness may be entirely inappropriate. To say, however, that some evil deeds are simply unforgivable does not capture the complexity and richness of all the social contexts within which gross evil is committed. In South Africa, for example, where the language of "reconciliation" has defined the way in which that society is beginning to deal with its traumatic past, many stories of forgiveness have indeed emerged. And in Rwanda, although the "r" word, "reconciliation," was taboo for several years after the 1994 genocide against Tutsis,[12] and although the international tribunal in Arusha was pursuing more conventional remedies centered on the principle of punitive justice, the government has established a National Reconciliation Commission. It has also worked out a program to release Hutu prisoners so they can be brought to a traditional form of justice, *gacaca,* which, it is expected, will promote truth telling and hasten the rehabilitation of those who have committed genocide into society. Thus, while there may be value in recognizing and posting the limits of forgiveness, if such exist, some societies are finding it more constructive to focus on discovering and nurturing the conditions that make forgiveness first conceivable, then ultimately possible.

Of course, in order to set conditions for forgiveness, it does indeed bear asking: When someone has committed the kind of radically evil acts that Arendt had in mind, what does it mean for the person to express regret? How do we judge the genuineness of that remorse? How do we know that the signs of alleged contrition are not simply a product of the perpetrator's having been caught, or of changes within the society that have destroyed his power base and support structures and have left him vulnerable? Specifically, how do we know that were a de Kock to step magically today into a time machine that took him back to apartheid South Africa, he would not disembark from it right back into his garments of warfare to wage destabilization against blacks? How can one tell that such remorse is not merely "witness stand" remorse that suddenly is forthcoming because, with no way out, the accused wants moral leniency?

One set of questions — the how-can-we-know questions — has to do with verifiability. A second set has to do with the moral possibility itself — the psychological and epistemological possibility — of achieving authentic remorse in the wake of having performed the unthinkable.

"After such knowledge, what forgiveness?" T. S. Eliot asks in "Gerontion."[13]

Both sets of questions are real and both are legitimate. Yet it remains equally legitimate that when perpetrators do in fact express regret or guilt or contrition, however it may be ascertained, what seems to lie, as Nicholas Tavuchis has put it, "beyond the purview of apology"[14] can in fact be transformed from an unforgivable deed into a forgivable one, into "this has happened and we must find ways to move forward." Philosophical questions can and should give way and be subsumed to *human* questions, for in the end we are a society of people and not of ideas, a fragile web of interdependent humans, not of stances.

Not all the victims who appeared before South Africa's Truth and Reconciliation Commission were willing or able to forgive those who had so deeply violated their integrity. Yet lessons from the TRC proceedings, approached with an open mind — and heart — can help us chart a path along which forgiveness may occur, as well as the conditions that make it difficult, or even morally inappropriate, to forgive. On the one hand, to dismiss perpetrators simply as evildoers and monsters shuts the door to the kind of dialogue that leads to an enduring peace. Daring, on the other hand, to look the enemy in the eye and allow oneself to read signs of pain and cues to contrition or regret where one might almost have preferred to continue seeing only hatred is the one possibility we have for steering individuals and societies toward replacing long-standing stalemates out of a nation's past with genuine engagement. Hope is where transformation begins; without it, a society cannot take its first steps toward reconstructing its self-identity as a society of tolerance and coexistence.

What happened at the Truth Commission may not be generalizable to all other situations. But what the work of the TRC suggests is that cycles of political violence can indeed be broken and that there are alternatives to revenge and retributive justice. Much more work needs to be done in South Africa. True social transformation — and healing of victims — will come about only if the issues of economic justice and the myriad problems that post-apartheid South Africa faces are addressed.

An important condition for the possibility of democratization after totalitarian rule is the forging of a vocabulary of compromise and tolerance, especially in the aftermath of mass tragedy. For the exercise of forming that vocabulary is part of the project of creating the operating rules of the democratic game, since democracy — and democratization — necessarily involves settling differences through the politics of contestation and compromise among equals, which is different from the goal of simply preserving law and order or of making sure that people remain or are put where they belong. The latter set of imperatives seeks to protect the privileged, and their property, against encroachments; the former process seeks to create new relationships and repair old ones. One of the challenges a political community faces in seeking to make the transition into a properly functioning democracy is therefore to create conditions that encourage replacing enmity with, if not love or friendship, then at least regard for others as fellow humans. For the absence of empathy, whether at the communal or personal level, signals a condition that, in subtle but deeply destructive ways, separates people from one another. When criminal offenders, even of the most egregious kind, show contrition and apologize, they are, quintessentially, *acting as human beings.*

What enables some victims to forgive heinous crimes? What distinguishes them from those who feel unable to do so? In addition to an external context that makes reconciliation normative through the language of restoration — a truth commission, for example, or a counseling agency that focuses on victim-offender encounters, or a national dialogue that begins to put in place the symbols and vocabulary of forgiveness and compromise — there are internal psychological dynamics that impel most of us toward forming an empathic connection with another person in pain, that draw us *into* his pain, regardless of who that someone is. The possibility of making an empathic connection with someone who has victimized us, as a response to the pain of his remorse, stems significantly from this underlying dynamic. The power of human connectedness, of identification with the other as "bone of my bone" through the sheer fact of his being human, draws us to "rescue" others in pain, almost as if this were a learned response embedded deep in our genetic and evolutionary past. We cannot help it. We are induced to empathy because there is something in the other that is felt to be part of the self, and something in the self that is felt to belong to the other.[15] Empathy feels *with* the other in a reciprocal emotional process in which one asks for it, or his very situation seems to ask for it, and the other responds by offering it.[16] Empathy reaches out to the other and says: I can feel the pain you feel for having caused me pain.

This is not a statement about whether it "makes sense" for the victimized to respond with empathy, nor an evaluation of the propriety of extending forgiveness. It is a tracing of what makes it possible for enemies to connect in a way that might otherwise seem unimaginable.

There is another dimension to the internal dynamic that motivates many to connect with those who have victimized them. A broad consensus exists in the literature that in order to torture, kill, and maim, perpetrators must first exclude their victims from the moral obligations they feel toward the world in general and, in particular, toward those with whom they are socially and politically connected.[17] Moral exclusion of a victim from the community of those who deserve to be treated humanely, in effect, effaces his pain. It makes it unreal or, as Elaine Scarry has written, "invisible, inaudible."[18] When perpetrators express remorse, when they finally acknowledge that they can see what they previously could not see, or did not want to, they are revalidating the victim's pain — in a sense, giving his or her humanity back. Empowered and revalidated, many victims at this point find it natural to extend and deepen the healing process by going a step further: turning around and conferring forgiveness on their torturer.

The motivation to do this does not stem only from altruism or high moral principles. The victim in a sense *needs* forgiveness as part of the process of becoming rehumanized. The victim needs it in order to complete himself or herself and to wrest away from the perpetrator the fiat power to destroy or to spare. It is part of the process of reclaiming self-efficacy. Reciprocating with empathy and forgiveness in the face of a perpetrator's remorse restores to many victims the sense that they are once again capable of effecting a profound difference in the moral community. Victims may have been able to function quite well in other contexts, but in this one area, at those moments when something reminds them of this one person, this one ordeal, they feel dehumanized again, halved and ineffective, quarantined in an area of their mind and of their life where they remember being told in effect that they do not matter, that the moral obligations ordinarily extended toward others do not apply in their case. It is to seal these cracks in their psyche — cracks that they sometimes unexpectedly reencounter — that many victims discover within themselves an inexorable movement toward forgiveness at the moment when the person who represents their pain drops his facade of indifference and opens up to express contrition.

Far from being an unnerving proposition and a burdensome moral sacrifice, then, compassion for many is deeply therapeutic and restorative. The psychological compulsion that makes us identify with and want to rescue others in severe difficulty and the desire to be rehumanized by someone who has denied our humanity are such powerful emotional dynamics that they can drive many victims to forgive and to enter into a constructive encounter with the offender, even when their internal moral compass points toward the inappropriateness of doing so and the offender seems morally undeserving.

Some have argued that forgiving perpetrators is particularly inappropriate because many of them *choose* not to see the victim's pain, or even enjoy inflicting it and, in a gruesome display of sadism, take pleasure in monitoring the victim's bodily reactions and responses as they fail one by one. But it is not the particular psychological path the offender took to overcome his inhibitions about causing another person pain — or rendering that pain invisible or irrelevant — that matters in this dynamic of remorse and forgiveness. What matters is the recognition that in the past lies a nightmare and in the future, the possibility of regaining one's sympathetic instincts.

In addition, in a totalitarian society where power structures exert a tremendous influence on how and what one thinks, the relationship between personal choice and societal pressure is not straightforward. Add to this a deeply stratified society, such as racially divided South Africa, where, starting well before one's capacity even to make moral choices has been tested, one's sense of moral obligation toward others is rigidly channeled along lines of "us" versus "them," and the images of the "them" depict a group that exists only as objectified others. Then, choosing to value or not to value another takes on an even more layered meaning.

When perpetrators feel remorse, they are recognizing something they failed to see when they violated the victim, which is that victims feel and bleed just like others with whom they, the perpetrators, identify. Remorse therefore transforms the image of victim as object to victim as human. Through the narrative of truth — of telling the story of how a human life was destroyed — a murdered victim is "resurrected" to affirm his or her humanness. At the same time, remorse recognizes the pain of the surviving family members. To illustrate my point about the humanization of the victim, let me return to what Doreen Mgoduka, the widow of one of de Kock's victims, said: "De Kock is the only one who helped us retrace the steps of what really happened. You have no idea how much of a relief knowing the truth about my husband was. De Kock brought us the truth so that we can be with our husbands, understand what happened to them and then release them again." Referring to her husband, she said, "Now I can mourn properly because this has helped me retrace his steps in life in order to let him go in death."

For de Kock, dredging up the memory may well have been an uncomfortable experience, or even a banal one. To Mrs. Mgoduka, however, de Kock's words seemed to *reconstitute* her husband — to bring him back again — so she could "be with" him awhile and lay him to rest herself. Beneath the surface of the TRC hearings, beneath the level of mere verbal exchange, something else was going on that constituted a powerful transfer of inner realities between killer and victims' relatives. In these situations, the killer's words are, in a sense, performative utterances, almost palpably potent instruments that accomplish the reorganization of the survivor's inner reality even as they come out, regardless of how flat, shifty, or uninspired they may sound. It is not the mannerisms the killer might use in speaking them that makes his words so powerful; it is the very fact that he is saying them at all. The words are what the victim wants to hear, to touch. *The words* themselves.

In another memorable hearing before the TRC, John Ackerman turned to the killers of his wife, members of the armed wing of the Pan-African Congress, the APLA (Azanian People's Liberation Army), and said: I want you to turn around and face me and tell me how it happened. I want you to apologize "in your own language."

Ackerman had already acknowledged the apologies the men had made through their written submissions to the Truth Commission. What he wanted now went beyond apology. Like Doreen Mgoduka, Ackerman wanted to hear their words directly in a personal "I-thou" encounter, and he wanted to receive them in their most authentic form, "in your own language."

Ackerman's wife had been killed in 1993 during an armed attack on St. James' Church, a predominantly white church in Cape Town. The APLA's motto was "one settler, one bullet."

After each of the APLA members responsible for what came to be known as the St. James' Massacre had spoken directly to him and apologized, Ackerman wanted to know if they specifically recalled, out of all the white worshippers who had died that Sunday, the woman who was his wife and how she had been killed. He wanted them to say, "Yes, she was sitting over there, we remember her; we remember what we did to her," to reconstitute her and her last moments through language, to reinstate her memory as a living, distinct, individual human being and mother and wife, not just another dead "settler."

From his seat on a higher level of the floor behind the men, Ackerman prodded their memory: "My wife was sitting next to me in the front pew. She was wearing a long blue coat — " His voice began to crack as he finally broke down and began to weep. "I want you to tell me if you saw her," he said. "Do you remember firing at my wife? If you don't remember I will accept it, but I want to know if you saw her, if you remember firing at her."

The perpetrator cannot restore what he has irrevocably damaged, but his words can go beneath the scar tissue left by the trauma, put its elements back into play, and thus help the victim master the memory of it.

But even forgiveness does not necessarily bring finality because it does not erase the past. Closure is not always possible, as Martha Minow reminds us.[19] But through forgiveness a provisional vocabulary of reconciliation, if not friendship, is created. To give this vocabulary greater permanence and lend it a multiplier effect through the larger society, it needs to be reinforced at the level of political leadership. In a nation recovering from sustained political conflict and internecine war, governmental and party members must do more than set aside the language of enmity. They need to move beyond mere talk about "peace" and "forging ahead" in "our great nation" and begin to demonstrate actual commitment to solving the hard problems of a community still learning to talk to itself, a community in which mistrust has become second nature.

Just as the Truth Commission's records, and accounts such as Elie Wiesel's *Night* and John Conroy's *Unspeakable Acts*,[20] offer evidence that ordinary people, under certain circumstances, are capable of far greater evil than we could have imagined, so are we capable of far greater virtue than we might have thought. Societal groups *can* transcend cycles of violence and forgive, if not necessarily fully reconcile with, other groups. But that uncertain process is made more likely, and less tentative, when it is supported by an ethos of acknowledgment and accommodation and underpinned by the nationally constructed language, cues, and symbols of collective reconciliation. The result may not be reconciliation in its full sense. But through the vicarious experience of stories of forgiveness, a society can begin to heal itself, and a more authentic and lasting sense of self-esteem and of collective worth can come to permeate public discourse about the past.

Epilogue

In SEPTEMBER 2002, de Kock's lawyer, Schalk Hugo, and I went to see him at Pretoria Prison, where I had not been since July 2000. I could have gone on my own, but that would have counted as part of de Kock's annual quota for social calls he was permitted. I needed the official status of Hugo's office, too, in order to guarantee a conversation with de Kock in a private consulting room. Arrival at the Pretoria Correctional Service cells was far less complicated than it had been on my previous visits; I felt disoriented. As I was wondering what had changed, Hugo explained that de Kock had been moved to the "local" section. His status had been upgraded to A, which placed him in the category of exemplary prisoners.

After entering the prison through two ordinary-looking doors, with no warders escorting us, we found ourselves in a small, rectangular reception area in which there were two stools. A bench was on one side of the room, and a counter separated the visitors' side from a black guard. The guard greeted us through thick iron bars that ran above the counter and chatted and joked with Hugo. I perched on a stool Hugo had pulled out for me, and watched as he went through a routine that he no doubt had accomplished many times: writing down our names in the visitors' register; reaching out to take some forms, which he then filled in; asking the guard where we were going to meet de Kock; and making sure that someone had gone to call de Kock. His meeting with the prisoner was going to be brief, Hugo told the guard, but mine would be longer.

De Kock soon entered the room, on the other side of the bars. He was wearing a green prison uniform that resembled the one he'd worn at amnesty hearings. I remembered his first appearance at the hearings for the Motherwell bombing, in 1997 in New Brighton Township in Port Elizabeth. He had inspired the black audience filling the great hall to spontaneous applause during his testimony that day when he named his superiors and lashed out at them for not having "the backbone to stand up and take responsibility."

De Kock greeted Hugo and me with a wave and a smile. Behind the smile and his thick black-rimmed glasses, I could see signs of wear and perhaps of sadness. A moment later we met in the office to which we had been assigned. He extended his hand to me before taking his place across from us. Hugo engaged in some small talk, handed him some documents to sign, and left. Looking at de Kock more closely, and watching him talk, I was sure I saw evidence of sorrow. It had been more than eight years since his arrest, trial, and conviction, and five years since his first appearance before the TRC. He had been granted amnesty for all his crimes except the two for which he was serving a double life sentence, a sentence he was hoping would be reversed by presidential pardon. Hugo's intention to apply for clemency on de Kock's behalf had been widely reported. But Hugo had been reluctant to discuss the details of the application with me. I didn't probe. I had politely refused to give him a copy of the manuscript of this book when he had asked to see it.

"What's in your heart?" I asked de Kock when we were alone. Earlier he had seemed to avoid looking directly at me. When our eyes did meet, I was reminded of something he'd said during my preceding visit. We'd been sitting in a small and frigid courtyard, with two armed white prison guards about three yards away, wearing heavy brown coats and busy with their own conversation. "What are my chances, Pumla?" de Kock had asked. "I mean, is there hope for me?" Then, the TRC hadn't announced its decision concerning his amnesty plea. It was as if he were begging for an answer, any answer I could provide; as if my yes or no would somehow resolve matters for him.

Now the same question hung unmistakably in the air between us. He had submitted his petition for pardon to the president, he said. All he could do was wait. "What else can I do?" he said.

What he *had* done was to request a transfer from a cell next to inmates who he claimed were promoting right-wing ideology among Afrikaners in prison. "I just couldn't stand them anymore," he said. "We were arguing all the time. I told them their thinking is off, it's dangerous. I don't want a war again. I don't ever want to go back to where we were. That time has passed. I'm not interested in their politics. I want to make that clear." De Kock said he had been moved to a part of the prison where he could mix freely with black inmates, including members of the ANC and PAC.

It was obvious that he wished to show unambiguously that he was pursuing a higher course than the prisoners who were advocating hatred. "I think the people reviewing the petition I've submitted to the president know this," he said. He told me that he had been invited to testify before the Defense Intelligence Committee, and based on the information he had provided, nobody in the present South African government could doubt his commitment to restoring peace in the country in whatever way he could. He was more worried about what the attitude of "the people" was: "What concerns me is how the black community will receive any positive outcome that might result from my application," he said.

Interesting, I thought, that he seemed to recognize the profound pain and destruction he had caused, not only to the victims of his actions, but also to an entire society oppressed by the system for which he had fought by whatever means necessary.

De Kock made an extraordinary contribution to the TRC process, a point that is acknowledged in the commission's final report. Most of the security police and certainly all the police generals who applied for amnesty were forced to do so as a result of de Kock's disclosures to the commission. Some of these men had been convicted of their crimes, and had failed in their bids for amnesty, yet they still walk free. Gideon Nieuwoudt, whose security department in the Eastern Cape came to notoriety for its role in the 1977 death of Black Consciousness leader Steve Biko, is one of these. There is an element of injustice in this. De Kock, of course, does not have a strong claim on justice. He does, however, have a claim on our understanding and compassion.

De Kock's hope for release from prison increased when, in May 2002, thirty three political prisoners who had been serving sentences for crimes committed in the anti-apartheid struggle were freed by presidential decree. President Mbeki's decision in these cases sparked heated debate over the unfairness of showing mercy only to perpetrators at one end of the political spectrum. In the midst of the intense response to the president's action, the justice minister brought up the possibility of a blanket amnesty. Such a law would effectively liberate all prisoners incarcerated for politically motivated crimes, from the left and the right, and it would set aside the criminal prosecution of many security policemen and police generals who had been refused amnesty by the TRC. Some people strongly objected to this on the grounds that it would lead to an undoing of the work of the Truth Commission.

South Africa is at a difficult juncture in its transformation, where extreme right-wing politics is threatening to emerge as a serious menace. To avoid letting loose a group of vengeful men, any act of pardon should transcend the usual political significance of such gestures. It should take seriously the issue of whether perpetrators of gross human rights abuses have faced their past and reflected on the moral implications of their actions. If this is not done, a blanket pardon may lead to a reversal of what set South Africans on a crucial path of transition. Some perpetrators of right-wing crimes remain unchanged and continue to hold their old attitudes. Conservative Party member Clive Derby Lewis, for example, who is serving a life term with Polish right-winger Janusz Walus for the murder of the former South African Communist Party leader Chris Hani, made his attitude clear before the TRC: "How can I apologize for an act of war? War is war."

The challenge, I think, is how to define morally reasonable grounds on which to grant perpetrators mercy and allow them to go free. These should include evidence of remorseful regret and a commitment to efforts aimed at ensuring that South Africans never fight one another again in a war. People who fail to see the senselessness of the bloodshed of the apartheid regime, who dishonor the dead, who haven't learned to grieve for the violent loss of so many innocent lives, should be watched closely. Mercy should be granted cautiously. And yet society must embrace those who, like Eugene de Kock, see and even lead on the road of shared humanity ahead. Our capacity for such empathy is a profound gift in this brutal world we have created for one another as people of different races, creeds, and political persuasions.

Appendix
 A Short History of Apartheid
Notes
Acknowledgments
Index

Appendix
A Short History of Apartheid

THE UNION OF South Africa (whose founding could be seen as a form of reconciliation following the Anglo-Boer War between the Boers, or Dutch, and the British), established in 1910, institutionalized the total exclusion of blacks from participation in political life. Political equality for blacks, declared the powers that be, was not merely undesirable; it was "an absurdity." Membership in parliament was limited to white males. Blacks in the Cape had the franchise, but by 1936, under an act that established separate representation for blacks, black Africans were removed from the voters' rolls and were allowed only three white representatives in parliament. By the time apartheid came into existence in 1948, processes aimed at removing blacks not just from constitutional politics but from citizenship itself had begun.

The foundations for apartheid were laid in the policies outlined by a commission set up in 1905 by the British High Commissioner in South Africa, Sir Alfred Milner. Asked to come up with strategies to deal with the "Native question," the commission proposed segregation between black and white, and the creation of "locations" for blacks on the fringes of the cities and towns.[1]

Noel Mostert, in his "epic" of South Africa's past and the shadow it cast on the future, reports that the recommendations of the commission echoed the British High Commissioner's own views that "[y]ou only have to sacrifice the 'nigger' absolutely, and the game is easy."[2]

The "sacrifice" of black people was codified into law as apartheid after the electoral victory of the National Party in 1948. The National Party (NP) drew its membership from Afrikaners and had a strong basis in Afrikaner nationalism. The party enjoyed a significant majority in parliament, which grew even larger in the 1970s and 1980s, that is, during the period when anti-apartheid opposition was at its peak. The NP's bedrock goal was racial, cultural, and political purity, that is to say, a society based on *apartheid* — literally, separateness. The effect of apartheid was not only to legalize all forms of discrimination against blacks — forced removals, demolition of homes, life in "locations" and in arid Bantustans (Group Areas Act, 1950); economic exclusion through reserving jobs for whites; inferior education (Bantu Education Act, 1953); pass laws and racial classification (Population Registration Act, 1950); and laws that enforced total separation of blacks and whites in public and in private (Prohibition of Mixed Marriages Act, 1949) — but also to disenfranchise blacks and reduce them to second-class citizens.

The African National Congress was founded in 1912 to campaign for non-racial democracy and human rights, which black people were denied in the colonial era. The ANC was revived and popularized as a people's liberation movement in the 1940s with the formation of the ANC Youth League, led by Walter Sisulu. The Freedom Charter, which was adopted in 1955, became the ANC's blueprint for a vision of a South Africa that "belonged to all who live in it — black and white." For decades the ANC used peaceful forms of protest. But then came the event that shocked the world, on March 21, 1960, when several thousand unarmed black people gathered in the Vereeniging township of Sharpeville and marched to the police station to protest the hated pass laws, and the police opened fire on the crowd — an incident that came to be known as the Sharpeville Massacre. Countrywide protests erupted, and a number of civil suits against the government followed. The government responded by declaring a state of emergency and banning all anti-apartheid organizations, and then passed laws, effective retrospectively, exonerating police from responsibility in acts committed against those involved in the peaceful march. Thus began a pattern of laws that served to silence anti-apartheid opposition while empowering the police to commit acts of violence. In the same year the government banned the Pan-African Congress and the ANC.

Thousands of people were arrested. Through its string of repressive legislation, the government rendered every conceivable act of opposition an act of treason and strengthened its police and security structures. The Bureau of State Security (BOSS), a security branch that was given immense powers and the extraordinary task of "protecting the country," was established. Arrests and detention of members of political organizations continued throughout the 1960s. In 1963, Justice Minister B. J. Vorster appointed as head of BOSS General Hendrik van den Bergh, who was later to tell a commission, "I have enough men to commit murder if I tell them, 'kill'!" One suspects that this became the mantra of the South African security force over the years. One of the most notorious government initiatives at the time was the recruitment of black and white collaborators,[3] who frequently infiltrated the liberation movements at home and abroad. This strengthened the security department's network, leading to the identification, capture, and sometimes assassination of black and white anti-apartheid political activists.[4] The government's informers created terror, suspicion, and divisiveness within the movement. This led to internal investigations that often resulted in the torture and murder of suspects.

After the Sharpeville Massacre, both the PAC, which had organized the Sharpeville anti–pass law protest, and the ANC concluded that the actions of the apartheid regime called for an end to forty-eight years of peaceful protest. Force had to be answered with force. Nelson Mandela announced the establishment of Umkonto we Sizwe (Spear of the Nation, MK for short), an armed wing of the ANC with Mandela as its commander in chief, to carry out acts of sabotage. The early phase of the armed struggle, as described by Joe Slovo, was "controlled violence" directed against government installations.[5] A police raid on the MK's secret headquarters on Rivonia farm in Johannesburg on July 11, 1963, and a lengthy trial that ended the following year on June 12, led to life sentences for Mandela, Sisulu, Kathrada, Goldberg, and four other leaders of Umkonto we Sizwe.

In 1963 parliament passed legislation that enabled the police to detain people for a maximum of ninety days without trial. State repression spun out of control; hundreds of thousands of apartheid's opponents were detained while thousands were severely tortured and often died in detention, particularly in the mid-to-late 1970s. When the state security police were not able to convict political activists in the courts, they used covert methods of killing, or simply killed overtly and claimed they were rooting out ANC terrorists. More discriminatory laws were passed following the June 1976 police massacre in Soweto of more than five hundred students involved in a peaceful demonstration against the "Bantu Education" laws, and especially against the use of Afrikaans as a medium of instruction in black schools. The end of the 1970s saw another wave of bannings of political organizations aligned to the black consciousness movement, and an exodus of young people who sought a home in one of the two political organizations in exile, the ANC and PAC, swelling the ranks of the armed wing of the liberation movement.

In 1977 P. W. Botha, who was then prime minister, launched his notorious "Total Strategy," although it wasn't until 1983 that Botha's plan was implemented. Total Strategy was designed to counter what Botha termed the black liberation movement's "total onslaught" by preserving apartheid and ensuring the continuation of white supremacist policies. It was a plan coordinated at the highest level, which would have political, economic, military, and psychological components.

In 1983 Botha took the first step — the establishment of a new parliament that allowed for power sharing among whites, "coloreds," and Indians but excluded blacks from participation in government. For blacks, the government created a separate system of black "counselors" who were given formal authority, but little real power or support, to manage the affairs of their urban areas. In the view of many blacks in the communities they were supposed to govern, the counselors had no mandate as leaders.

In the concerted effort that ensued to dismantle this separatist arrangement, the anti-apartheid struggle launched the United Democratic Front (UDF), a coming together of more than five hundred political organizations charged with a national campaign for redressing local grievances. One of the main vehicles of protest the UDF introduced was consumer boycotts of white-owned stores and other businesses. A common theme of the boycotts, often effective on one level, was the ruthless disciplinary measures that blacks who broke ranks or those suspected as police collaborators could expect. Extremely violent methods of dispensing with those perceived to be "enemies of the people" — including so-called necklace killings — emerged. Blacks killing other blacks powerfully served one of the functions of the Total Strategy, which was to destabilize the liberation movement.

The maintenance of "law and order," which apartheid South Africa's security forces always claimed was their goal, became increasingly blurred under Total Strategy implementation by corrupt state activities, including outright murder.[6] Concrete results against opponents of the state were expected regardless of how they were achieved. "The crucial thing was to get the job done," de Kock had said in one of our interviews, explaining the core principles of Total Strategy. "The question of whether what we did was legal or not did not come into the picture. How we did it was not important. The results were."

But under the guise of going after the ANC, the police and army killed many more ordinary unarmed black citizens than liberation movement fighters.[7] Beginning in 1983, a consensus began to form in the ANC that unless the resistance to the regime of terror shifted into a higher gear, the cause might never prevail. More and more liberation fighters of the ANC were infiltrating the country, and Umkonto we Sizwe stepped up its bombing campaigns in South Africa.

State-orchestrated violence escalated during the 1980s, when covert operations units were established in the security police and defense departments, which ran a network of police informants (black and white), murder squads, and scientists skilled in the art of biological warfare. South Africa saw an increase in widespread torture by security police, the disappearance of political activists, mass killings, and the mysterious deaths of detainees and others, which usually occurred under direct instruction from, or with the full knowledge of, police generals. Most of the police "investigations" of these incidents were simply cover-up operations. At the same time, the police were given immense powers and immunity, with many laws on the books that protected them from prosecution for the human rights abuses they committed.

By the end of the 1980s, President F. W. de Klerk and his colleagues were driven to the realization that the days of apartheid were over; it was time to introduce a more inclusive citizenship in the statute books. On February 11, 1990, he released Nelson Mandela from prison. A widely representative commission, the Congress for a Democratic South Africa (CODESA), was established to negotiate what amounted to a transfer of power to the majority, which resulted in the election of Nelson Mandela and the ANC as the ruling party in April 1994. A major concern of CODESA was how to deal with the past in a way that would break the cycles of violence, bring about social cohesion, and restore peace. The result was the establishment of the Truth and Reconciliation Commission.

Notes

2. An Encounter with "Prime Evil"

1. See Appendix.

2. Riaan Bellingham was involved in many other covert murders, most notably the killing of seven young activists from Gugulethu Township in Cape Town (see Iris Films Academy Award–nominated film *Long Night's Journey into Day*), which he masterminded. In February 2002 Bellingham was granted amnesty for his role in the killing of the Gugulethu Seven.

3. Interview with Pearl Faku, Port Elizabeth, October 1997.

4. Christopher Browning, *Ordinary Men: Reserve Police Battalion 101 and the Final Solution in Poland* (New York: Harper Perennial, 1993), p. xx.

5. Cited by Ron Rosenbaum, *Explaining Hitler: The Search for the Origins of His Evil* (New York: Harper Perennial, 1999), p. 395.

6. Ibid., p. 195.

7. In our attempts to understand perpetrators, our explanations are often tied up with empathy for them. One factor pulling us toward empathy rather than antipathy is that in the final analysis, perpetrators are human like us. Another factor is our role as

thinking, language-making creatures; in the search for explanations of the grim acts of destruction that fill the pages of history books, we believe that the dynamism of language can provide us with some answers.

8. The C-Max model of maximum security prisons was the brainchild of Khulekani Sithole. The former commissioner of correctional services appeared on South African national TV to refute reports by prison warders that Eugene de Kock was a model prisoner. "How can de Kock be a model prisoner?" he asked. "Eugene de Kock has an evil profile" (SABC *Special Report*, November 2, 1997). Sithole was forced to resign from his position in 1999 after he was found guilty of a number of crimes, including (among others) corruption, organized crime, sexual harassment, and mismanagement (Andre Jurgens, "Rotten to the Core," in *Sunday Times*, March 5, 2000).

9. In subsequent visits to the prison, the guards told me that de Kock had not shown any signs of dangerousness in prison and that he was the least of their problems in C-Max, but the prison officials nevertheless had to treat him like a dangerous criminal for two reasons. First, the prison made no distinction between ordinary criminal violence and state-sponsored violence. Unlike liberation fighters, who could petition for political prisoner status, de Kock had been charged, tried, and convicted as a common criminal. The other, perhaps subtler reason why de Kock was *treated* as dangerous was to foreclose any evidence that might disprove the claims that he *was* dangerous.

10. The Broederbond has not escaped the changes in South Africa; now it is called the Afrikanerbond and continues to function as a cultural organization to promote the interests of the Afrikaans-speaking community. Its membership is no longer secret, and women and people of color have been allowed to join.

11. See Appendix.

12. Peter Z. Malkin and Harry Stein, *Eichmann in My Hands* (New York: Warner Books, 1990), p. 213.

13. The bombings and mass shootings conducted by the state's covert operations army and police units at houses believed to be inhabited by liberation fighters in neighboring countries. Often the targeted houses were home to whole families. Visiting neigh-

bors' children were often injured or killed during these operations. The cross-border operations then served a double purpose: to track down and kill liberation activists and their "fellow travelers," as well as to provoke the wrath of the communities within which the liberation activists lived.

14. Nic van Rensburg ordered the attack on the Chand house in April 1990 (see Jeremy Gordin, *A Long Night's Damage: Working for the Apartheid State* [Johannesburg: Contra Press, 1998]). Van Rensburg was also involved in the murder of other activists — Sizwe Kondile and the Cradock Four (Martin Meredith, *Coming to Terms: South Africa's Search for Truth* [New York: Public Affairs, 1999]). Van Rensburg was refused amnesty for his role in the Motherwell bombing.

15. The issue of high-ranking ANC members who informed for the apartheid government came up during the TRC hearings. A PAC member of parliament, Patricia de Lille, publicly demanded that the ANC reveal the identity of the informants, and she mentioned names of suspected ANC police spies. Joe Mamasela, a former member of the Vlakplaas death squad unit, also told the TRC that some senior ANC members had come to Vlakplaas in a helicopter. De Kock, however, dismissed Mamasela's helicopter story as "wishful thinking" and "dangerous disinformation."

16. Crimes de Kock committed as head of the apartheid government's covert operations are recounted by de Kock in shocking detail in Jeremy Gordin, *A Long Night's Damage.*

17. One may notice the inconsistencies in de Kock's behavior and begin to suspect that his feelings of remorse were faked to earn sympathy. But there is an explanation for the apparent contradictions. De Kock, like many perpetrators, had enjoyed commanding fear and power. The commission's public hearings turned the tables and reversed the roles between perpetrator and victims. So de Kock, like others in his position, would revert to his old attitudes now and again, partly as a way of reclaiming the power he once wielded.

18. These men were deserting Vlakplaas at a time when a commission of inquiry, the Harms Commission, was being set up to investigate the existence of death squads operating from there.

De Kock was obviously afraid that the *askaris* who were deserting, and those who, like Ngqulunga, couldn't cope with the pressure of the investigation and possible public exposure, might have leaked information about the nature of the operations conducted at Vlakplaas and about the identity of its officers and *askaris*.

19. De Kock had not yet been appointed to head Vlakplaas, but nevertheless he played an active role in this incident. For example, he suggested the use of a limpet mine to ensure that the leader of COSAS, who he thought could identify his men from Vlakplaas, was killed in the incident.

20. All the men mentioned in connection with this incident, except former minister of police Louis Le Grange, applied for and were granted amnesty for their roles in the plot.

21. As in the case of the Gugulethu Seven. See *Long Night's Journey into Day*.

22. There is enough evidence to suggest that General Johan van der Merwe and General Johan Coetzee had put pressure on de Kock and his men. Both generals had been police commissioners and were implicated in criminal activity against opponents of the apartheid state (see Meredith, *Coming to Terms*; Gordin, *A Long Night's Damage*; Terry Bell, *Unfinished Business: South Africa's Apartheid and Truth* [Observatory, Cape Town: Redworks, 2001]; Antjie Krog, *Country of My Skull: Guilt, Sorrow, and the Limits of Forgiveness in the New South Africa* [New York: Random House, 1999]), and both applied for amnesty for their crimes.

3. The Trigger Hand

1. In the film *The Silence of the Lambs*, from the novel by Thomas Harris, Hannibal Lecter (Anthony Hopkins), the evil psychotherapist in prison for murder and cannibalism, befriends a young investigative agent, Clarice Starling (Jodie Foster), and enjoys making disturbing statements that penetrate her psychological defenses and touch raw emotions. At one point he makes momentary contact with her hand through the bars of his cell. It is left to the viewer to imagine what he is thinking; but the mo-

ment is a chilling one because of the pathological relationship Lecter has had with human flesh. It is the question mark left by the touch that makes the scene so chilling. What is its meaning for him? Is it sexual? A power move? Sheer psychological torture? And for her?

2. See Albie Sachs, *Soft Vengeance of a Freedom Fighter* (Los Angeles: University of California Press, 2000).

3. I was surprised to learn that Sachs held this conciliatory attitude long before anyone thought that the "new" South Africa would be arriving anytime soon. George Bizos, counsel extraordinaire, whose role in many inquests during the dark days of apartheid led to his book *No One to Blame?*, writes that in 1988 Albie Sachs had already started to advocate peace. During a discussion at Columbia University on what was to be done about those who committed gross violations of human rights, an ANC member stood up and challenged Sachs's views about peacemaking. Sachs remarked that calls for revenge "would delay the dawn of freedom." "'Comrade,'" Sachs implored, "'if I can forgive them, I am sure many more will do so.'" George Bizos, *No One to Blame?* (Cape Town: David Phillip, 1999).

4. The Evolution of Evil

1. Although questions about conscience are best addressed through the examination of the behavior of individual perpetrators, the "little men" at the bottom of the hierarchy (Christopher Browning, *Ordinary Men: Reserve Police Battalion 101 and the Final Solution in Poland* [New York: Harper Perennial, 1993], p. 27), this should be balanced with the study of the extent to which individual factors are influenced by social and political processes. A perspective that integrates both individual and group dimensions will have greater explanatory power than one that focuses solely on one or the other.

Social identity theory (see Henri Tajfel, *Differentiation between Social Groups: Studies in the Social Psychology of Intergroup Relations* [London: Academic Press, 1976]; Henri Tajfel and John Turner, "The Social Identity Theory of Intergroup Behavior," *Annual Review of Psychology,* 33 [1986]: 1–39) has been used to explain how individuals, through self-identification with the groups to which they belong, are drawn into violent behavior against people defined as "other." The construction of "otherness" is an essential step on the path toward the destruction of victims. "Enemies of the state," "the Antichrist," "terrorists," and "communists" are some of the terms often used to create the language of hatred, which is then deployed to justify violently harming those outside one's own group. Zygmunt Bauman (*Modernity and the Holocaust* [Ithaca, N.Y.: Cornell University Press, 1989]) suggests that such definitions split the population into "the marked and the unmarked." Those who are marked are the ones who are excluded from society's moral obligations and targeted for "special" treatment; and "what is proper in relation to 'ordinary' people must not necessarily be proper" in relation to those targeted (p. 191).

Psychoanalytic group theorists (e.g., Alfred Bion and Elliot Jacques) clearly spell out the mechanism by which "others" lose the moral protection that normally prevents individuals from harming other human beings. Using the psychoanalytic concepts of splitting and projective identification as a framework, they argue that these behaviors of splitting and projecting unwanted parts of the self are accentuated in a group, and are particularly heightened in the context of a violent group, where the ego goes through a process of depersonalization, ego depletion, and a reduction in the ability to think rationally. Thus, there is a loss of self-awareness, a decline in the capacity for private reflection and for critical moral reflection. This explains in part why perpetrators — at least those who had a conscience before it was silenced at the time they committed atrocities — once separated from their groups, either through imprisonment or abandonment by their leaders, are able to reflect on their past actions with shame and even remorse.

2. Clearly the churches were a support to the ideology and status quo of apartheid. But there was also a substantial ecumenical group of clergy and Christians who were a powerful force for change. One key event was the World Council of Churches conference in Cottesloe in 1960, at which the Afrikaans Church,

the Nederduitse Gereformeerde Kerk (NGK), was a participating member. There was an effort by the Council of Churches to get the NGK to renounce the policies of the apartheid government as heretical. Although there was some indication that the NGK might do so, the Broederbond and the government placed enormous pressure on the church to back off. The NGK then retracted its intentions, except for Beyers Naude, one of a handful of Afrikaner voices to speak against apartheid. G. McLeod Bryan, *Voices in the Wilderness: Twentieth-Century Prophets Speak to the New Millennium* (Atlanta: Mercer University Press, 1999).

There was a great deal of suspicion in the Afrikaans press before the Cottesloe Consultation began. Peter Randall reports that a secret circular criticizing the conference was sent out by the Broederbond in January 1961, and Prime Minister Hendrik Verwoerd declared that the Cottesloe Consultation was "an attempt by foreigners to meddle in the country's internal affairs." The pressure seems to have been significant. "Certainly many members of the NGK began to be afraid merely to be seen in the company of 'Cottesloe men.'" Peter Randall, "Not Without Honour: The Life and Work of Beyers Naude," in *Not without Honour: Tribute to Beyers Naude*, ed. Peter Randall (Johannesburg: Ravan Press, 1982), p. 22. The NGK finally withdrew from the World Council of Churches and was further isolated when the larger international association, the World Alliance of Reformed Churches, declared apartheid a heresy in 1982 (Bryan, *Voices*).

Beyers Naude became editor of the journal *Pro Veritate*, which was devoted to exposing the truth about apartheid's evil. In 1963 an NGK synod passed a motion that called on its members not to participate in *Pro Veritate*'s efforts. Peter Randall reports that fellow Broederbonders gave "friendly warnings" to Naude about his involvement with the journal ("Not Without Honor," p. 22). Naude's experience demonstrates how the government treated those church leaders who did speak out against apartheid. He was harassed by police raids on his home and office, interception of his mail, phone taps, revocation of his passport, and secret service surveillance. In 1973 Naude was brought to trial for refusing to testify before a parliamentary committee investigating "subversive" activities. The type of social and political pressure that Naude and others underwent is illustrated in Bryan's commentary: "It was clear the government would not tolerate Naude or the Christian Institute [of which Naude was director] much longer. The Afrikaners so detested him that at his own mother's funeral his kin locked arms to prevent him from standing at her graveside" (*Voices*, p. 40). In 1977, in a sweeping roundup of opposition leaders and organizations, Naude received a five-year banning order, which severely restricted his movements, and the Christian Institute was shut down. One key event in Naude's life was his decision to withdraw formally from his membership in the NGK and to join the black NGK in Afrika. In the late 1970s politicians and military leaders, such as General Magnus Malan, then chief of the South African Defense Force, were beginning to frame for white society what the government meant by "total strategy," calling upon all to participate in apartheid's war. Malan said: "The war is not only an area for the soldier. Everyone is involved and has a role to play." *Johannesburg Star*, September 10, 1977.

3. The effects of violence can be quite traumatic for both children and adults. Trauma is a state in which the ego is so overwhelmed that it is forced to employ defense mechanisms to avoid immensely distressing material. One of the best-known psychological mechanisms used to cope with early childhood trauma is identification with the aggressor. Such a response, however, would seem to contradict the very basis of the theory. How can identifying with the perpetrator of an unpleasant event be a strategy for coping with its distressing features? How does this notion fit in with the ego's "pleasure principle," its goal of avoiding unpleasant states of mind? In his book *Beyond the Pleasure Principle*, Sigmund Freud (and see Anna Freud, *The Ego and the Mechanisms of Defense*, vol. 2 [New York: International University Press, 1936]) explains how the victim of a traumatic event, by reversing the roles, converts the experience of helplessness into one of action. Thus, by stepping into the shoes of the aggressor, the victim regains the power that was lost in a moment of helplessness. According to Judith Herman (*Trauma and Recovery: The Aftermath of Violence — From Domestic Abuse to Political Terror* [New York: Basic Books, 1992]), the repetition of the trau-

matic experience is an attempt at mastery and integration of the trauma.

Current psychological discourse has recast the theory of identification with the aggressor into the shame hypothesis, which holds that experiences of helplessness, powerlessness, and trauma in early childhood are inextricably interwoven with a violent lifestyle in adulthood. See J. V. Caffaro, "Identification and Trauma: An Integrative Developmental Approach," *Journal of Family Violence*, 10 (1995): 23–40; H. P. Blum, "The Role of Identification in the Resolution of Trauma," *Psychoanalytic Quarterly*, 56 (1987): 606–627; Donald G. Dutton and Susan K. Golant, *The Batterer: A Psychological Profile* (New York: Basic Books, 1995); James Gilligan, *Violence: Reflections on a National Epidemic* (New York: Vintage Books, 1997); Bob Wallace and Anna Nosko, "Working with Shame in the Group Treatment of Male Batterers," *International Journal of Group Psychotherapy*, 43 (1993): 45–61; Nicole Woelz-Stirling, Margaret Kelaher, and Lenore Manderson, "Power and the Politics of Abuse," *Health Care for Women International*, 19 (1998): 289–301.

4. Jeremy Gordin, *A Long Night's Damage: Working for the Apartheid State* (Johannesburg: Contra Press, 1998), p. 45.

5. Ibid. De Kock related an incident during which one of his parents' quarrels led to his mother driving away in her car. He noted that he had never experienced the kind of fear he felt when he watched his mother leaving, "not during battles, not during riots, not during fistfights" (p. 46). Yet when I saw de Kock's face for the first time in a newspaper photograph, I thought that he still had that frightened little boy's appearance. Seeing his brother on TV several weeks later, I saw the same look.

6. Ibid.

7. Gilligan, *Violence*.

8. The "dangerous living" in this constant repetition of violence has been associated with individuals who have not confronted or successfully integrated their trauma. Freud referred to this as "repetition compulsion," which he conceptualized as an attempt to master the original traumatic experience. Trauma evokes a complex set of emotions. It is conceivable that the repeated acts of violence are also an attempt to escape these over-

whelming emotions through splitting and projection, and thus take on a life of their own. As Richard Rhodes has written, "Repetition is the mute language of the abused child . . . like the resonances of a temple drum that aren't heard so much as felt in the heart's cavity" (*A Hole in the World: An American Boyhood* [New York: Simon & Schuster, 1990], p. 267).

9. Richard Rhodes, in his memoir recounting his psychological and physical brutalization in early childhood, skillfully and painfully details his and his brother's childhood trauma. They, and many others who have suffered abuse as children, escaped becoming violent adults because of "timely intervention. Someone saw their suffering and had the courage or simply the generosity of spirit to intervene. . . . [T]hey were supported, or given reason to believe that they were valued, or shown alternatives to violence — nonviolently coached" (Rhodes, *A Hole in the World*, p. 322).

10. Although there are no conclusive statistics on the number of abused children who turn out to be violent adults, data showing that a certain percentage of them do end up being abusers themselves are quite compelling, with men more likely to be involved in violent behavior than women. See Elaine Carmen, Patricia Perri Rieker, and Trudy Mills, "Victims of Violence and Psychiatric Illness," *American Journal of Psychiatry*, 141 (1984): 378–383.

11. Tina Rosenberg, *The Haunted Land: Facing Europe's Ghosts after Communism* (New York: Random House, 1995), p. 66.

12. To say that perpetrators *choose* violence and therefore they alone must carry the burden of responsibility oversimplifies the issue of choice in instances of state-sanctioned violence, and in a society where the rules of morality exclude those targeted by the state. James Gilligan (*Violence*) suggests that where there has been a "tragic flaw" in society, the law has no right to mete out tough justice to violent individuals. That the deep structure of a corrupt political state and its social institutions often produce individuals like de Kock cannot be contested. But this does not mean that perpetrators' moral — or legal — blameworthiness is reduced because of society's collective guilt. The question exists

whether perpetrators could have chosen not to join the army or the police in a totalitarian state. Some look back and realize that they did have options, that they could have made decisions that would have enabled them to avoid becoming part of the state's machinery of destruction. For victims, no such choices existed. Lawrence Langer refers to any notion that victims might have chosen otherwise as a "choiceless choice" (*Holocaust and Human Behavior* [Brookline, Mass.: Facing History and Ourselves Foundation, 1994], p. 351).

13. Richard Rhodes, *Why They Kill: The Discoveries of a Maverick Criminologist* (New York: Knopf, 1999), p. 322. Rhodes maintains, however, that it is indefensible to argue that people are violent because of some psychological condition. I think that the wellsprings of violence are not as clear-cut as he suggests. Many theories have been proposed and many models developed, but none of them have been able to answer this vexing question. In contrast to Rhodes's view, Gilligan (*Violence*) takes the extreme position and advocates an approach that reduces the blameworthiness of perpetrators of violent acts. He is highly critical of laws that execute extreme forms of punishment without an attempt to understand, in the sense of appreciating the *meaning* of, brutal and serious crimes.

14. F. W. de Klerk spoke at the Kennedy School on February 14, 2001. My question to him was: "Eugene de Kock has said that he is bitter 'at all those who gave me orders   yet the person who sticks most of all in my throat is former president F. W. de Klerk.' Is it your view, sir, that it is unreasonable for a man who was secretly funded by the state and rewarded with medals to lay some of the blame for his actions on the head of state?"

15. The State Security Council was composed of all cabinet ministers and heads of intelligence, police, and security. De Klerk, as minister of education, was a member of the SSC and then served as its chair once he became president.

16. Justice Quartus de Wet at the Rivonia trial that was held from July 1963 to June 1964, where Mandela, Walter Sisulu, Ahmed Kathrada, Denis Goldberg, and others were found guilty of sabotage.

17. Kennedy School of Government, February 14, 2001.

18. Craig Williamson had collaborated with Eugene de Kock in other covert operations, notably the bombing of the ANC's London offices in 1982, which, according to Williamson's testimony to the TRC, had been authorized by General Johan Coetzee. At a TRC hearing in September 1998, Williamson sought amnesty for his role in the killing by letter bomb of Ruth First and Jeanette and Katryn Schoon. Jeanette Schoon and Marius Schoon, her husband, who had been a political prisoner for several years, were anti-apartheid activists living in exile in Angola. A parcel bomb sent to Marius Schoon in Lubango, Angola, where he was a university professor, killed his wife and daughter.

Ruth First, the indefatigable anti-apartheid campaigner and member of the South African Communist Party, had left South Africa in the 1960s after enduring several detentions under apartheid's repressive security laws. She was killed by a letter bomb sent to her office in 1982 at the Eduardo Mondlane University in Maputo, Mozambique, where she was director of the Center for African Studies. First was married to Joe Slovo, army commander of the military wing of the ANC (see Appendix) and the minister of housing in South Africa's first democratically elected government. For detailed background on First's life, see the book written by her daughter, Gillian Slovo, *Every Secret Thing: My Family, My Country* (London: Abacus, 2001). In Slovo's book, Craig Williamson makes this reference to his involvement in First's murder: "I was in the loop that killed your mother" (p. 265).

19. Armed forces hearings, October 9, 1997, Cape Town.

20. George Bizos, *No One to Blame? In Pursuit of Justice in South Africa* (Cape Town: David Phillip Publishers, 1999). Leonard Knipe, the policeman who investigated the killing of the Gugulethu Seven, who were trained by Vlakplaas *askaris* in the use of firearms and explosives and then lured to a trap where they were killed by the police, admitted to the TRC that his investigation was flawed but didn't tell the commission that it had been part of a deliberate cover-up scheme.

21. Armed forces hearings, October 9, 1997, Cape Town.

22. Ibid. The Nazis also used euphemism. The difference — an important one — is that they used this sanitized language to project an image of scientific professionalism. The "Final Solution"

was presented as a historic act of social engineering that had to be undertaken to purify and improve the German gene pool, a policy about which even (German, Aryan) children were encouraged to be fanatically proud, and this "objective" language was employed to enhance the rational-bureaucratic efficiency by which the grand policy was to be carried out. "The 'objective' attitude — talking about concentration camps in terms of 'administration' and about extermination camps in terms of 'economy' — was typical of the S.S. mentality, and something Eichmann, at the trial, was still very proud of." Hannah Arendt, *Eichmann in Jerusalem: A Study of the Banality of Evil* (New York: Penguin, 1994), p. 65. Euphemism and high language were used not so much to hide the feeling that there was something wrong with the program as to dissociate it from tawdry, pedestrian aspirations. Apartheid's leaders, by contrast, resorted to euphemistic phrases not only to hide their intent from others and to stave off legal repercussions but also to shield *themselves* psychologically from their true intentions.

23. Arendt, *Eichmann*, p. 93.

24. Ibid., p. 95.

25. Peter Z. Malkin and Harry Stein, *Eichmann in My Hands* (New York: Warner Books, 1990), p. 214.

26. Ibid., p. 220.

27. Evidence did emerge of a plan being hatched in some sectors of the military to use biological weapons to destroy blacks. Wouter Basson, known as "Dr. Death," who was on trial for masterminding South Africa's biological warfare program, and against whom damning evidence was given by former military personnel, was nevertheless acquitted on all charges against him in April 2002.

28. Gitta Sereny reports that when Frantz Stangl, who was a commander at Treblinka, joined the Nazi Party, he had to renounce his membership in the Catholic Church (*Into That Darkness: From Mercy Killing to Mass Murder* [London: Pimlico, 1988]).

29. Psalm 18:47–48.

30. Zygmunt Bauman argues that the probability that the moral oddity of one's action will ever be a painful moral dilemma

is small in a system that glorifies atrocities, and moral conflict rarely arises (*Modernity*).

31. I am indebted for this formulation to conversations with Franklyn Ayensu.

32. In addition to prison terms, stiff fines were imposed on those who refused military service. A maximum of six years' imprisonment and a fine of six thousand rand could be reimposed each time military service was refused.

33. *Hansard*, August 1970. According to an MP in Botha's National Party, Dr. Morrison, conscience should never be made the highest priority, and taking into consideration the issue of human rights and freedom of conscience was "wreckless." *Hansard*, March 1972.

34. The bloody political chaos that has plagued what is now known as the Democratic Republic of Congo since the end of Belgian colonial rule played a part in the South African government's propaganda message that a black government in South Africa would lead the country to ruin.

35. In a speech to parliament on May 29, 1985, Defense Minister Magnus Malan left no doubt what those results were expected to be. "I want to make it clear again," he said, "I make no apology for doing so, that we shall do everything possible to sniff out and locate the ANC and take action against them wherever they may be . . . and however we like" (*The Star*, Johannesburg).

36. Morgan Scott Peck argues that there is what he terms "fragmentation of conscience," which results in no one person's holding himself or herself accountable for the behavior of the group. "Whenever the roles of individuals in a group become specialized, it becomes both possible and easy for the individual to pass the moral buck to some other part of the group. In this way, not only does the individual forsake his conscience but the conscience of the group as a whole can become fragmented." Morgan Scott Peck, *People of the Lie: The Hope for Healing Human Evil* (New York: Simon & Schuster, 1983), p. 218.

37. The psychiatrist James Gilligan suggests that fear is incompatible with violence: "What is most startling about the most violent people is how incapable they are, at least at the time they commit their violence, of feeling love, guilt, or fear" (*Vio-*

lence, p. 113). It is not inconceivable, however, that perpetrators experience fear in situations where they might be killed themselves. Also, I would argue that fear is one of the complex themes that define the internal world of people who lead lives of violence. At a deep psychological level, fear and violence are two sides of the same coin: violence overcomes the fearful and troubling elements of shame.

38. When Gitta Sereny (*Into That Darkness*) asked Frantz Stangl, a commander at Treblinka, if he remembered the faces of his victims, he said he couldn't. Sereny concluded that Stangl had so dehumanized his victims that in his eyes they no longer existed as human beings.

39. Robert Lifton has also advanced the notion of "doubling," in which the perpetrator operates in terms of a double self, whereby one part of the self "disavows" the other: "What is repudiated is not reality . . . but the meaning of that reality." Nazi doctors knew that they were participating in the policy of "selection" of Jews for the gas chambers. But they did not interpret "selection" as murder. Robert Lifton, *The Nazi Doctors: Medical Killing and the Psychology of Genocide* (New York: Basic Books, 1986), p. 422.

5. The Language of Trauma

1. Most of the seventeen commissioners were divided between the Reparations Committee and the Human Rights Violations Committee, with only two serving on the Amnesty Committee, which was composed of judges and senior members of the legal profession. The Amnesty Committee was by law (National Unity and Reconciliation Act) required to be chaired by a judge, and amnesty decisions did not need the endorsement of the full commission, as was the case with decisions made in the other two committees.

2. It's not clear why victims of police killings were chained and placed under police guard in hospitals. This may have been done for swift arrest and questioning after their release or, more likely, to make sure that they didn't speak to the press.

3. The limitations of language in communicating traumatic experience has been observed by many scholars who write on victims' testimonies (see Lawrence Langer, *Admitting the Holocaust* [New York: Oxford University Press, 1995], and Susan Brison, *Aftermath: Violence and the Remaking of a Self* [Princeton, N.J.: Princeton University Press, 2002]). But I think that there is a danger in laying too much emphasis on verbal language in that this ignores other forms of communication that victims might inadvertently "choose" when they find words inadequate. Body language is one. Silences are another. For example, when a victim suddenly stops speaking, or starts to cry at a particular point in the testimony, or when the victim's voice breaks, these are not just moments of absence of language but representational expressions (or "acts") that may tell us more about what the traumatic experience meant then, and means now, for the victim than words ever could.

Some victims have tried to use images to express their deepest emotions about their trauma. But the historian Lawrence Langer cautions that this too may not be enough. Langer has dealt extensively with the subject of the inadequacy of language as a vehicle for communicating trauma, most notably in his two books *Admitting the Holocaust* and *Holocaust Testimonies: The Ruins of Memory* (New Haven, Conn.: Yale University Press, 1993). In *Holocaust Testimonies* he points out the incompatibility of certain imagery used in literary works with actual experiences in Nazi death camps, and notes that this "underlines the difficulty of finding vocabulary of comparison for such an incomparable atrocity" (p. 19).

Elie Wiesel also speaks about the chasm between what is remembered and how it is retold: "Ask any survivor; he will tell you, he who has not lived the event will never know it. And he who went through it will not reveal it, not really, not entirely. Between his memory and his reflection there is a wall — and it cannot be pierced" ("Art and Culture after the Holocaust," in *Auschwitz: Beginning of a New Era?* ed. Eva Fleischner [Washington, D.C.: KTAV Publishing, 1977], p. 405).

4. Martha Minow, in her book *Between Vengeance and Forgiveness: Facing History after Genocide and Mass Violence* (Bos-

ton: Beacon Press, 1998), suggests that being able to testify, despite the limitations of language, is a triumph for the victim: "[E]ven to speak, to grope for words, to describe horrific events, is to pretend to negate their unspeakable qualities and effects. Yet silence is also an unacceptable offense, a shocking implication that the perpetrators in fact succeeded" (p. 5).

5. Lawrence Langer evokes Thomas Mann in referring to this impossibility of closure as a "bottomless layer of incompletion" (*Holocaust Testimonies*, p. 23). There cannot be a final and complete "reconstruction" of trauma. Yet each version told by the victim reflects the various phases of progression with the traumatic material — or regression, depending on the intensity of experiences that reawaken the trauma in the victim's life and the resources available to deal with them — and is true to the victim's experience.

6. Maurice Friedman, "Why Joseph Campbell's Psychologizing of Myth Precludes the Holocaust as Touchstone of Reality," *Journal of the American Academy of Religion*, 66 (1998): 385–401.

7. Primo Levi, "The Memory of Offense," in Geoffrey Hartman, ed., *Bitburg in Moral and Political Perspective* (Bloomington: Indiana University Press, 1986), pp. 130–137.

8. Daniel Abramson, "Make History Not Memory: History's Critique of Memory," *Harvard Design Magazine*, 9 (1999): 1–6.

9. From a paper, "The Rupture of Silence," which I presented for the Rama Mehta Lecture, sponsored by John Kenneth Galbraith at Radcliffe College on March 21, 2000. The paper was published as "Traumatic Memory," in *Truth and Lies: Stories from the Truth and Reconciliation Commission in South Africa*, ed. Jillian Edelstein (New York: New Press, 2001), pp. 25–31.

10. Langer, *Holocaust Testimonies*, p. 19.

11. Mr. Mkabile's intuition was probably accurate. During a break shortly after his testimony, one of the white commissioners came up to me and said she had been "scared" for a moment that Mr. Mkabile would actually open his fly. Strange, I thought, that she could imagine a man who had told a story of such moral courage capable of crudely exposing himself before the TRC. I couldn't help thinking how deeply entrenched the boundaries that divided black and white were in South Africa. I knew Mr.

Mkabile, both as a "father" from my hometown and as the respectable head of the household I had visited in preparation for the public hearings where he was going to testify. For my white colleague, I thought, Mr. Mkabile evoked all the stereotypes assigned to black people, and she was unable to recognize in reality the dignity of victims, which supposedly drove the work of the TRC.

There is another possible interpretation of my colleague's reaction. Langer points out that by its very nature, traumatic testimony induces horror, confusion, and disbelief in the hearer. "The more painful, dramatic, and overwhelming the narrative, the more tense, wary, and self-protective is the audience, the quicker the instinct to withdraw" (*Holocaust Testimonies*, p. 20).

12. Dori Laub, "Bearing Witness or the Vicissitudes of Listening," in Shoshana Feldman and Dori Laub, *Testimony: Crises of Witnessing in Literature, Psychoanalysis, and History*, (New York: Routledge, 1992), 57–92.

13. Under the TRC mandate, "gross human rights violations" were defined as violent acts against individuals committed with a political motive, including killing, abduction, torture, and severe ill-treatment of any kind.

14. For instance, General Johannes Viktor, who was commanding officer when thirty-nine ANC marchers were killed while demonstrating against General Oupa Gqozo, who was the leader of the nominally independent homeland of Ciskei and considered to be one of the homeland puppets of the apartheid government, appeared before the TRC to answer questions concerning his role in the incident. At the public hearing, Viktor maintained that he had done nothing wrong, and that he had acted properly since the marchers were posing a threat to the stability of the Ciskei government. When I asked him if he had any words for the family members of the victims, who were seated in the front row in the audience facing him, he responded that he saw no reason to address them. Concerned about the effect I thought his attitude would have on the family members, I accused Viktor of callousness and insensitivity. Two other commissioners, Bongani Finca and Mapule Ramashala, were enraged by Viktor's harsh words. Ramashala referred to Viktor's statement

as "outrageous." My remarks and Finca's and Ramashala's angry outbursts prompted criticism from Max du Preez in his weekly TV "special report" on the TRC. He accused us of violating the TRC mandate of evenhandedness. Although the incident had passed unnoticed by the mainstream press, after du Preez's comments it became a major news story. Archbishop Desmond Tutu asked us to apologize, and then issued a statement. At the time, I didn't see our reaction to Viktor as violating the TRC mandate. He was not applying for amnesty. We were not making a judgment about his guilt or innocence. I felt we were upholding the spirit of the act by responding in a manner that took into account the victims' feelings. The hearing was, after all, a victims' hearing, and the act required that the TRC ensure that victims were treated with sensitivity, dignity, and respect — in other words, that they be protected from the callousness of insensitive witnesses.

15. At a meeting of the Western Cape region of the commission, I proposed psychological debriefing sessions after each round of public hearings for all TRC members — commissioners, committee members, and staff. A colleague, Trevor Lubbe, was appointed on a volunteer basis to assist with this process. While senior members attended only one debriefing session, TRC staff continued to attend group sessions with Lubbe for some time. Many of the staff, particularly statement takers and investigators, who were the first contacts victims had with the TRC, had to deal with victims' raw emotions.

16. In George Bizos, *No One to Blame?* (Cape Town: David Phillip, 1999), pp. 219–220.

17. Personal communication, March 1998, Cape Town.

18. The critically acclaimed documentary on the TRC, *Long Night's Journey into Day,* by Frances Reid and Deborah Hoffman, illustrates the full range of responses from forgiveness to vengefulness.

19. Nicholas Tavuchis, *Mea Culpa: A Sociology of Apology and Reconciliation* (Stanford, Calif.: Stanford University Press, 1991), p. 27.

20. The notion of "settlement" evokes legal connotations. There is growing discussion of the use of apology in the court-

room, and some states, such as Massachusetts, have laws that encourage and make it possible for defendants to apologize if they
need to while protecting them from the possibility of further in-
criminating themselves. Lee Taft discusses the challenges inherent in the use of apology in the legal setting in "Apology Subverted: The Commodification of Apology," *Yale Law Journal*,
(March 2000): 1135–60.

21. Mary Hunt, "Apologies Are in Order," *WaterWheel*, 13
(2000): 1–2.

22. Dori Laub, "Truth and Testimony," *American Imago*, 48
(1991): 85.

23. Pumla Gobodo-Madikizela, "Remorse, Forgiveness, and
Rehumanization: Stories from South Africa," *Journal of Humanistic Psychology*, 42, no. 1 (Winter 2002): 7–32.

24. "Psychological trauma is the affliction of the powerless."
Judith Herman, *Trauma and Recovery: The Aftermath of Violence — From Domestic Abuse to Political Terror* (New York: Basic Books, 1992), p. 33.

25. Taft, "Apology Subverted."

26. Paula N. Nesbitt, "Forgiveness as a Reflection of Social
Inequality," in *Church and Society* [January/February 1999]:
pp. 55–39. Nesbitt acknowledges that forgiveness may be "harder
to enact for those in social locations of dominance than for those
in the margins" (p. 57). Some have criticized Christian values for
fostering passivity and resignation in victims. Jeffri Murphy and
Jean Hampton, in the introduction to their book *Forgiveness and
Mercy* (New York: Cambridge University Press, 1990), put it this
way: "Christianity had encouraged the development of meek and
forgiving dispositions that will tolerate oppression, and that will
call that toleration virtue." I see it differently and would suggest
that for victims who have been subjected to years of abuse, powerlessness may evoke forgiveness, not the other way around.

6. Apartheid of the Mind

1. I couldn't help noting the irony in someone with German
roots saying she "knew nothing" about the operations that had

taken place on a farm right next to hers. I wondered if perhaps she'd come from Namibia, where many German farmers lived for decades until that country obtained its independence in 1990.

2. Brian Mitchell was sentenced to death after being found guilty of the killing of eleven people at Trust Feed in KwaZulu-Natal in December 1988. His sentence was commuted to thirty years after the April 1994 South African election. The killings, carried out by policemen acting on Mitchell's orders, were intended to target ANC supporters. The people killed, however, were supporters of Inkatha Freedom Party, the conservative black political organization that often staged joint attacks with apartheid forces against the ANC. Mitchell applied for and was granted amnesty by the TRC in December 1996. He became a regular news item for being among the first perpetrators of gross human rights abuses to receive amnesty. Mitchell's wife reportedly left him in the midst of the public focus on his case.

3. We suspected that there were many whites who had unresolved questions about conscription and about the war that their sons had fought in the black townships and in the neighboring states. If Mrs. McGregor and others like her would tell their stories in public, we hoped that their testimony would encourage whites in general to identify with the TRC process, which many white people regarded as a witch-hunt and an attack on whites.

4. I left the TRC in April 1998 and went to the United States to take up a summer research fellowship at the University of Michigan to finish writing my Ph.D. dissertation, which I had had to put on hold for the two years I served on the commission. My original doctoral study was based on interviews with young black anti-apartheid activists who had committed "necklace" murders. As this represented the extreme of the liberation struggle, I decided to include the de Kock material in my study so as to examine the extremes of both sides of the political conflict, in particular the dynamics of politically motivated atrocities committed in the context of a group and state-sponsored atrocities committed by an individual.

Almost six months passed before I could look at the transcripts of my interviews with de Kock. My avoidance of the transcripts was symbolic of my inner struggle with the memory of those moments in my interviews with de Kock when I had felt a human bond with the man considered the most odious operative of the apartheid era. Finally, with the help of many people, I started to see my work on de Kock as culminating in two processes, one that would be purely scholarly (a Ph.D. thesis) and another that would be a deeply personal account of my conversations with de Kock — this book.

7. "I Have No Hatred in My Heart"

1. Peter and Linda Biehl have helped transform two men who were involved in their daughter's killing from murderers to responsible members of society. Ntobeko Peni and Easy Nofemela, who were members of the military wing of the Pan-African Congress at the time, were involved in the stabbing of Amy Biehl, the Stanford University student who was killed in Gugulethu, a Cape Town township. Peter and Linda Biehl came to Gugulethu to work with their daughter's killers. In applying for amnesty, Nofemela and Peni apologized to Peter and Linda Biehl, and in return the Biehls did not oppose their application. Peter Biehl opened his statement to the TRC with the following words: "We come to South Africa as Amy came, in a spirit of committed friendship, and to extend a hand of friendship in a society which has been systematically polarized for decades." The Biehls started the Amy Biehl Foundation in Cape Town, and Peni and Nofemela trained in one of the foundation's projects to become mechanics. I interviewed the Biehls about their relationship with Nofemela and Peni in June 2000. "I have no hatred in my heart," said Linda Biehl. "All I am concerned about is how these young men can reenter their community and rebuild their lives." Perpetrators who receive the gift of forgiveness are given a chance to change. Whether a perpetrator rises to the call or not may depend on a range of circumstances and opportunities for such change to take place. The Biehls offered their daughter's killers a second chance, and they rose to the challenge.

2. The United Nations tribunals are an important judicial

process for countries that have not dealt effectively with past human rights abuses. Their tendency to focus only on perpetrators on one side of a political conflict may, however, disrupt whatever fragile unity might be forged by two sides previously at war with each other. This could then fuel the anger of one side, which may feel that the law is biased against it as the "oppressor" group, when in fact there is often a record of human rights crimes committed by the oppressed group as well. The issue is not a simple one, for in recognizing that both sides produced victims, one may seem to be applying the same moral standard to the actions of the oppressor and those of the group that was fighting to end its oppression. But in societies trying to break the cycle of hatred and revenge, it is important first to acknowledge, as did the TRC, that human rights abuses were committed by both sides, and then to find an effective way of moving society forward. International tribunals target the "big fish" like Slobodan Milosevic, and rarely if ever shift their focus to crimes committed by dissident or victim groups. The problem becomes more complex when the victim group takes over power and, predictably, uses its "victim" status to gain public sympathy even for actions that may be undemocratic.

3. See Mary H. Rothschild, "Transforming Our Legacies: Heroic Journeys for Children of Holocaust Survivors and Nazi Perpetrators," *Journal of Humanistic Psychology*, 40 (2000): 43–55. Similar initiatives have emerged from this body of work, and some Jewish/German dialogue groups have broadened their focus to include participants from other conflict regions. For example, the TRT (To Respect and to Trust), a Jewish/German collective that was started by Dan Bar-On in 1990, has extended its principle of respectful relationship and brought together Israelis and Palestinians, Protestants and Catholics from Northern Ireland, and blacks and whites from South Africa. Another direct outcome of Dan Bar-On's peacemaking efforts has been a project that he cofounded with a Palestinian colleague, Sami Adwan, the Israel/Palestine peace research institute PRIME (Peace Research Institute in the Middle East).

4. The view that Holocaust memory has been exploited for financial gain and to deflect criticism of Israel and silence serious

questions about the Israeli-Palestinian conflict has been documented. Peter Novick (*The Holocaust in American Life* [Boston: Houghton Mifflin, 1999]) and Norman G. Finkelstein (*The Holocaust Industry: Reflections on the Jewish Exploitation of Jewish Suffering* [New York: Verso, 2001]) are among the most vocal critics of what Finkelstein has termed "the Holocaust industry." Finkelstein claims that the Holocaust "has proven to be an indispensable ideological weapon," and by deploying it "one of the world's most formidable military powers [Israel], with a horrendous human rights record, has cast itself as a 'victim' state" (*Holocaust Industry*, p. 3). The argument here seems to be that the status of victim continues to evoke public sympathy even when victims' circumstances have changed. Only when dialogue about the past recognizes the mutable roles of victim and perpetrator can we appreciate the potential for transforming innocence and guilt.

5. In this sense forgiveness, as a humanizing act, shifts our perspective from the traditional mode of blame to a higher level that requires perpetrators to take responsibility for the suffering they have caused others. At a public hearing on the Gugulethu Seven incident, a Vlakplaas-sponsored covert operation in which seven young black activists were killed after they were lured into a trap, the sister of one of the victims threw a shoe in the direction of the thirteen policemen who had been subpoenaed for questioning by the TRC. The woman had just seen her dead brother's mutilated body in a video shown at the hearing. All the policemen walked out in protest, threatening not to return to the hearings as their lives were "in danger." They saw the victim's sister's anger as closing off any possibility for dialogue. But this is only one way of looking at it. It is possible to see even an act of anger as an *invitation* to engage at a human level. The woman was saying, "Look at me, I'm bleeding inside over the horrible manner in which my brother died." Acknowledging her pain would have been a more constructive response to her mildly violent action. See the film *Long Night's Journey into Day* for some images of this incident.

6. Heribert Adam and I were part of a small group gathered for a weekend retreat in February 1998 on Goedgedacht farm in the

winelands region of the Western Cape to explore the possibility of establishing a think tank on reconciliation.

7. Albert Speer, Hitler's close ally, who was known as the chief architect of the Third Reich, is the only one who came close to showing what might be called remorse.

8. Richard Ramirez, dubbed "the Night Stalker" by the press, was arrested in August 1985 and charged with a series of crimes ranging from abduction to rape and murder. He was found guilty of thirteen murders and thirty other crimes and sentenced to the gas chamber. Ramirez met the freelance magazine editor Doreen Lioy after she started writing him letters. Their wedding ceremony was held at San Quentin in October 1996 (www.stage-direct.com).

9. ESMARELDA: What does it feel like?

BUTCH: What does what feel like?

ESMARELDA: Killing a man. Beating another man to death with your bare hands.

Butch pulls on his tee-shirt.

BUTCH: Are you some kinda weirdo?

ESMARELDA: No, it's a subject I have much interest in. You are the first person I ever met who has killed somebody. So, what was it like to kill a man?

BUTCH: Tell ya what, you give me one of them cigarettes, I'll give you an answer.

Esmarelda bounces in her seat with excitement.

ESMARELDA: Deal!

Pulp Fiction, 1994, http://www.godamongdirectors.com/scripts/pulp. shtml.

10. Perhaps this is the reason why Claude Lanzmann is fiercely opposed to analyses of the perpetrators of the Nazi Holocaust. Lanzmann is the producer of the film *Shoah*, which details testimonies of survivors of the Holocaust. All attempts to understand perpetrators represent for him "[w]hat I have called the obscenity of the very project of understanding." "The Obscenity of Understanding: An Evening with Claude Lanzmann, *American Imago*, 48 (1991): 480–487.

11. Hannah Arendt, *The Human Condition* (Chicago: University of Chicago Press, 1998), p. 241.

12. Erwin Staub, personal communication, June 19, 1999.

13. "Gerontion," in T. S. Eliot, *Selected Poems* (New York: Harcourt Brace Jovanovich, 1964), p. 34.

14. Nicholas Tavuchis, *Mea Culpa: A Sociology of Apology and Reconciliation* (Stanford, Calif.: Stanford University Press, 1991), p. 21.

15. H. Segal, *Introduction to the Work of Melanie Klein* (London: Hogarth Press, 1973).

16. Mary Rothschild articulated what giving an empathic response and making a humane connection involve from the point of view of someone whose parent was a Holocaust survivor. She described the remorse expressed by descendants of Nazi mass murderers and her response to it: "I felt compassion for the pain these people carried, not just for their families but also for the majority of Germans" ("Transforming Our Legacies," p. 49).

17. Zygmunt Bauman, *Modernity and the Holocaust* (Ithaca, N.Y.: Cornell University Press, 1989); Robert J. Lifton, *The Nazi Doctors: Medical Killing and the Psychology of Genocide* (New York: Basic Books, 1986); Erwin Staub, *The Roots of Evil: The Origins of Genocide and Other Group Violence* (New York: Cambridge University Press, 1989).

18. Elaine Scarry, *The Body in Pain: The Making and Unmaking of the World* (New York: Oxford University Press, 1985), p. 44.

19. Martha Minow, *Between Vengeance and Forgiveness* (Boston: Beacon Press, 1998).

20. Elie Wiesel, *Night* (New York: Hill and Wang, 1960); John Conroy, *Unspeakable Acts, Ordinary People: The Dynamics of Torture* (New York: Knopf, 2000).

Appendix

1. For an intriguing book on South Africa's past — and the continuities from that past — see Noel Mostert, *Frontiers: The Epic of South Africa's Creation and the Tragedy of the Xhosa People* (New York: Knopf, 1992). Data in this appendix were obtained from the epilogue to *Frontiers*. For more recent history, see

R. Hunt Davis, ed., *Apartheid Unravels* (Gainesville: University of Florida Press, 1991); and Heribert Adam and Kogila Moodley, *The Negotiated Revolution: Society and Politics in Post-Apartheid South Africa* (Johannesburg: Jonathan Ball, 1993).

2. Mostert, *Frontiers*, p. 1273. Mostert clearly illustrates that the British, who are often portrayed as "innocents" in the crime of apartheid, are as culpable as the Afrikaners.

3. Mark Behr, for example, an English professor living in the United States, confessed his role as an apartheid police informant at a conference, known as "Fault Lines," held in Cape Town in 1997. There was a torrent of angry criticisms of Behr in the press from other white former anti-apartheid activists, both for his betrayal and for what they considered an opportunistic apology. One of the most stinging criticisms was an article by Nick Borain whose headline screamed "The Smell of Rotten Apples!" a reference to Behr's book *The Smell of Apples*, a novel about a young Afrikaner boy growing up with the collective hypocrisy of an Afrikaner family and the society in which they live.

4. These activists included Neil Agett, Steve Biko, Richard Turner, and Dulcie September.

5. Joe Slovo, *Slovo: The Unfinished Autobiography* (London: Hodder and Stoughton, 1996). Slovo was the chief of staff of Umkhonto Wesizwe and the first minister of housing in the post-apartheid government. He was loved and respected by many South Africans for his lifelong anti-apartheid stand, and thousands of people went to the stadium in Soweto to celebrate his life and mourn his death in 1995 after his long battle with cancer.

6. At a hearing on May 7, 1997, Magnus Malan admitted having set up the Defense Force covert operations unit, the Civil Cooperation Bureau (CCB), to "penetrate and disrupt the enemy" in the mid-1980s. At a hearing on December 3, 1997, he conceded that the vague language used by generals in giving orders, as well as by politicians, was understood to refer to killing.

7. As part of the military component of the Total Strategy, the South African army was deployed for the first time inside the country, in the Eastern Cape townships. In Queenstown, the first "colored" commandos (in the terminology of apartheid, people of mixed race descent) were given training to join the counterrevo-

lutionary war the army was preparing to wage to silence black opposition in Mlungisi Township.

The idea behind establishing commando units was to maintain a continuity of white men's military responsibilities beyond their obligatory years of service in the army. The commandos were a white citizens' force drawn from a range of professions that included doctors, academics, and businessmen. They were often mobilized to join with the police and army, as the apartheid government's symbol of white unity, in enforcing the government's political, social, and economic goals. It was in the context of such joint military, police, and commando efforts that countless massacres of unarmed people occurred in the black townships of South Africa.

Acknowledgments

At the end of 1998, a few days after the Truth and Reconciliation Commission report was handed over to former president Nelson Mandela in South Africa, I presented material on this book at the Mary Ingraham Bunting Institute of Radcliffe College at Harvard University (now called the Radcliffe Institute for Advanced Research). Among the people in the audience was Deanne Urmy. After my presentation, Deanne came to me and asked me to consider writing a book. As my work evolved over the years, through lectures I gave at various academic institutions and human rights organizations in different parts of the world, Deanne offered me unfailing support and guidance. She has been a passionate and meticulous editor, and I am most grateful to her for her advice, insights, and ability to respond not only to the intellectual content of my work but to the emotional challenges of it. It has been an honor to work with her. I am also grateful to Martha Minow for introducing us.

In 2001 I was privileged to receive a grant from the United States Institute for Peace (USIP), and I am grateful to all the people there who helped me. The Episcopal Divinity School (EDS) in Cambridge, Massachusetts, was the institutional home for the grant, and I offer many thanks to Joanna Dewey, Ben Matlock, and Phillip Welton for their support in making this arrangement possible. Thanks also to Margaret Thorpe, the director of housing at EDS, who gave me sanctuary in a beautiful apartment in Cambridge.

This book was conceived in the ideal work environment of the Bunting Institute, where I spent 1998 and 1999 as a Peace Fellow, writing my doctoral dissertation. My journey to "the Bunting" began with e-mail in the summer of 1997 from my mentor and special friend, Leo Kamin, an honorary professor at the University of Cape Town's psychology department. The TRC was approaching its conclusion, and I needed a place to go to write my dissertation. Leo got in touch with Herbert Kelman, a psychologist and conflict resolution specialist at Harvard University, and asked about possible fellowships at Harvard. Herbert, whom I had met in 1993–1994 at Harvard, immediately contacted Rita Brock, the director of the Bunting. Rita Brock sent the Bunting fellowship application forms by courier to Leo in Cape Town. When they arrived, I was at my parents' home in a small village in the Eastern Cape, so Leo and his wife, Marie-Claire, flew from Cape Town to East London, a three-hour drive from my parents' home, to bring them to me.

I am deeply indebted to Leo Kamin. He and Marie-Claire helped me grapple with the analysis of my interview material, and it was by talking with them that I was able to articulate many of the questions I deal with in this book. They have been a source of great inspiration and encouragement.

I also wish to express tremendous gratitude to Herbert Kelman, who helped me through my first fellowship visit at Harvard and affirmed my work in my subsequent visits and throughout my stay in the Cambridge area. At the Bunting, Rita Brock was a crucial source of intellectual support. Her guidance and enthusiasm made me believe that my work was important enough to spend time discussing. Thanks also to Dan Bar-On for his insights and thoughtful comments at an early stage of my interviewing Eugene de Kock, and to Oscar Barbarin, who made it possible for me to spend the summer of 1998 at the University of Michigan, reading, reflecting, and struggling with the tapes and transcripts from those interviews.

The Bunting experience opened other doors, and I was privileged to spend two more years at Harvard, first at the Carr Center for Human Rights Policy and the Women and Public Policy Program at the Kennedy School of Government, and then at the Center for the Study of Values in Public Life at the Harvard Divinity School. I wish to acknowledge deep gratitude to Martha Minow, Swanee Hunt, Samantha Power, and Archbishop Desmond Tutu, without whose support these fellowships would not have been possible. Jonathan Shapiro, Sarah Moses, and Roger Falcon, whose research help was indispensable, were a gift.

Many others in the Boston academic community offered either critical comments on early drafts of this book or simply their encouragement. Among these are Roberta Apfel, Cynthia Cohen, Barbara Goldoftas, Judith Herman, Claudia Highbaugh, Mary Hunt, Michael Ignatieff, Tamar March, Nancy Nienhuis, Jill Reynolds, Bennett Simon, Lynn Andrea Stein, Phyllis Strimlin, Sherman Teichman, Dan Terris, Gale Yee, and Don Cutler, my agent. I wish to thank Swanee Hunt especially for organizing and providing space for the discussion of my work at various places, including her homes in Cambridge and Colorado, and for her extraordinary generosity and help. Special thanks to Sheila Sisulu, Claire Willis, Lisa DeLima, Abigail Erdmann, and Lulu Magunya, and to the many others, known and unknown to me, who have been part of this story and helped shape my thinking in important ways. I also thank those students at the Peace and Justice Department at Wellesley, the EPIIC program at Tufts University, the Episcopal Divinity School, and Harvard whose energy and ideas inspired my work.

I am grateful to the organizations that arranged gatherings and discussions, including Fran Colletti, Mark Skvirsky, and especially the director, Margot Stern Strom, at Facing History and Ourselves, and Mary Tiseo at South Africa Partners.

Thanks also to my friends for their constant encouragement: Ilona Anderson; Dorothy and Gaston Blom, friends of exceptional generosity; Rachel and Samson Munn; Meridel Rubenstein; Thina Siwendu; Nommso Stubbs; and Kaethe Weingarten, who kindly read parts of the manuscript at an especially busy time. Rob Riemen and Kirsten Walgreen invited me to speak at a conference on evil in the Netherlands in the summer of 2002, and it was wonderful to have an opportunity to extend the interest in my ideas to a broader audience. Thanks also to Albie Sachs, for reading the manuscript, for advising me, for affirming this book, and for showing me by example that this work matters. Franklyn Ayensu deserves special thanks for his careful reading of early drafts, for his patience, and for his questions and comments. I appreciate many people at St. Peter's Episcopal Church in Cambridge, especially the rector, Titus Presler; the director of adult education, Bill Edwards; and Douglas and Sally Craig Huber.

My greatest debt is to the people whose stories made this book possible: to Pearl Faku and Doreen Mgoduka for sharing their emotions and thoughts; to Eugene de Kock, for his willingness to be interviewed; to Tat'uMkhabile, Mam'uPlaatjie, Mam'uGishi, Mam'uKhuthwane, Anne Marie and Owen McGregor, John Ackerman, Linda Biehl, and Peter Biehl, whose work was the embodiment of the possibility of healing. It's been a privilege, and I'm very grateful.

Among people who gave me support when I started my interviews with Eugene de Kock, I remember with particular respect Archbishop Desmond Tutu, who has continued to support and encourage me. I thank also Zenzile Khoisan, who, as one of the first TRC investigators to interview de Kock, was willing to discuss his impressions before I met him. Dumisa Ntsebeza made the single greatest contribution by inviting me to submit my résumé to the TRC commissioners.

Many people were untiringly generous in helping my son, Bahle (Madik), cope with the isolation that my writing this book brought. My thanks to them, especially Fatima Mncube Barnes, Teddy Hunt Ansbacher, Douglas Du Cuito, and Shaun Godino.

I would also like to thank Amanda Heller, my manuscript editor, who with care and attention to detail helped to improve the text, and Liz Duvall, the manuscript editing supervisor, who took care of many last-minute details. Other people at Houghton Mifflin to whom I am grateful are Dan O'Connell, the publicist for my book, and Melissa Grella,, my editor's assistant.

My parents helped me find the courage to write this book, as they have done in all major ventures in my life. My thanks to them, to my sister Maud, to my brother Ngoza and his wife, Khuthala, and to my brother Mkhubukeli, for supporting me in every way they could. I owe more than I can say to my sister Sesi, who gave me a powerful intellectual connection with a person of graceful generosity and ethical strength. In late 2001, a few days before I went to South Africa to be with her during her last days, I spoke to her on the telephone. Her voice faint, she asked about the title of a talk I was about to give and went on to discuss my topic, bringing laughter to a serious subject in a way only she could have done. I was blessed to be able to join my family and Sesi's daughter, Nomusa, to be at Sesi's side for a few days before she passed away. It is to her that I dedicate this book.

Index